THE COOK'S COMPANION

A Dictionary of Culinary Tips and Terms

THE COOK'S COMPANION

A Dictionary of
Culinary Tips and Terms

•

FRIEDA ARKIN

Drawings by John Alcorn

Doubleday & Company, Inc., Garden City, New York

1968

Library of Congress Catalog Card Number 68–10546

First Edition

Contents

Introduction

"How *do you peel a tomato, for heaven's sake?"*

"Why does my cake have a hump in the middle?"

"My baked apples came out a mush! What kind of apples should I have bought for baking?"

"How on earth does one open an oyster?"

I can hear myself now. For someone who is the granddaughter of a chef, I came to marriage marvelously unprepared for kitchen combat. As a result of my earliest efforts my gallant husband uncomplainingly ate Bride's Biscuits (hardtack) and overdone steak (those times when we could afford steak) . . . and it was as much pity for him as memory of the succulent dishes of my youth which drove me to the telephone in anguish almost daily to beg my mother for enlightenment. She was one of five daughters who spent their growing years in their father's hotel kitchen, and it must have been the ease with which she diced and sliced, and boiled and broiled, and sent the most superb foods to our table, which made me take first-rate cooking for granted. I never had the good sense to learn directly at my mother's knee, alas—and I think it took a good ten years for me to make all the mistakes and all the calls for help which followed, of which this book is the outgrowth.

At that time I had in my kitchen a deep, wide drawer, and into that drawer went the variously scribbled scraps of paper, the memos written feverishly on the backs of torn envelopes, the jottings of all the hints and information I could glean from my disasters and inquiries. But finally there came a day when I could no longer close the drawer upon my last entry, it was so stuffed and heaped; and so I opened it wide and spread its entire contents out to the light of day. Why not arrange everything alphabetically, according to subject, said I to myself: the next time I roasted a duck, for example, I would know exactly what to do to keep the duck from being greasy and make certain it was tender to the bone, as well.

I realized then what it would have meant to me—and to my husband—and to the guests at our sometimes near-disastrous dinner parties—if I had had all this information at my fingertips years ago. The indigestion and tears which could have been avoided! The money saved! The fiascos which need not have occurred!

This book, then, I like to think of as a somewhat intensive course of study at mother's knee—a mother who knew her way around a kitchen blindfolded, who had only to put her hand to a sauce or a roast to make it behave as it should, who inherited from her father what the French call *tour de main*—we translate it here as "know-how." For she rarely, in my memory, had a cooking failure; nor was she ever at a loss for an explanation of the temperamental processes and reactions which surround a cooking stove or a mixing bowl.

Of course there are omissions. I have not had to tussle with every problem which can rear its ugly head in a kitchen. But here, two generations removed, are some of the fruits of my grandfather's labors in his kitchen, those fruits which came down to my mother and my aunts and my cousins and finally myself—for we are all, every one of us, kitchen slaveys out of love and good appetite.

The book is divided into two parts. The first, the main body of the book, consists of hints and tips about foods, their preparation, and various procedures in the kitchen, arranged alphabetically. The second section deals with cooking and menu terms, and I have attempted to include many new foods and items which we come in contact with today in our more and more cosmopolitan world of eating. Among the foreign terms there is, understandably, a predominance of French—but there are also many Italian, Spanish and German ones as well. I dedicate my labors to everyone who loves to cook, and to everyone (although I confess I cannot understand why) who hates it.

PART ONE

•

Culinary Hints

AN ALPHABETICAL ARRANGEMENT OF FOODS WITH HINTS AND TIPS ABOUT THEIR PREPARATION AND RELATED PROCEDURES

A

ALMONDS: one pound almonds with shells on equals 1 cup shelled equals 1¼ cups chopped equals 1½ cups ground.

to skin (blanch): drop shelled almonds into boiling water, turn off flame and let stand 3 minutes. Slip skins off and dry nuts on a clean dish towel.

ANCHOVIES:

in a sauce: mash an anchovy to a pulp and mix into any sauce for meat, fish or vegetables. There is no anchovy taste, but it gives a master touch to a gravy.

if too salty for some uses: soak in clear water 10 minutes, pat dry with a paper towel and immerse in clear olive oil until ready to use.

APPLES:

for applesauce: best apples for sauce are Jonathan, McIntosh, Cortland, Greening, Northern Spy, Gravenstein and Baldwin.

for baking: Jonathan, Northern Spy and Rome Beauty.

eating apples: preferred eating apples are Delicious, Golden Delicious, Winesap, McIntosh, Pippin, Stayman, Baldwin and Russet.

pie apples: Greening, Gravenstein and Northern Spy are generally the best pie apples, since a pie calls for a tart, firm-fleshed apple. Some people like McIntosh for their sweet spicy flavor, but these tend to soften during baking. To use soft-fleshed apples, cut slices thicker.

to keep apples from turning dark: rub cut surfaces with lemon juice, or soak in water to which lemon juice has been added.

ARROWROOT (see THICKENING)

ARTICHOKES (see also JERUSALEM ARTICHOKES):

to buy: pick firm, closed ones, not those with loose opened leaves.

to prepare: household gloves make handling easier. Snip off points of leaves with kitchen shears. Trim artichoke at base (stem end) and rub with lemon to prevent darkening before cooking.

to remove choke before cooking: force open center leaves from top and cut out choke with a curved grapefruit knife.

to cook: for added flavor, cook artichokes in broth instead of water. An artichoke is cooked if the leaves come off easily at a slight pull. Remove from liquid and drain by standing stem side up.

ASPARAGUS:

to buy: choose firm green stalks with hard-closed tips; avoid yellowed or limp asparagus. Asparagus continues to age and toughen after it has been cut, so the sooner you cook it after purchasing it the better.

to prepare: snap or cut off tough ends as far down on the stems as they will snap off cleanly. If stalks are thick, peel the lower portions with a potato peeler up to the tenderer part. Stand them with their stems in cold water to freshen for a half hour, before cooking.

to cook: asparagus can be cooked flat in a long narrow pan, but there is danger of overcooking the tips. It is better to tie them together in bundles of 8 or 10, or wrap bundles in cheesecloth for easy removal from water. Stand them in cooking water with their tips above water level. Cover pot during cooking—the tips will steam to softness while the tougher stems cook.

before serving: drain asparagus, then roll quickly in a dish towel to remove all water, then serve with or without sauce.

ASPICS AND GELATIN MIXTURES:

TIPS

- gelatin desserts sparkle twice as much when served in glass dishes than when served in china.
- rinse inside of mold with water before filling it with mixture to be jelled, to make unmolding easier. You can also grease the mold lightly first (use oil), but not if the aspic is a clear one—otherwise the grease will show.

to set: add a little more gelatin than is usually called for when making molded dishes, and they will be firmer when served.

- salads, desserts, pies, etc., can be made to set quickly by placing them in the freezer for about half an hour. Then remove and refrigerate.
- if you intend to add solids to a gelatin dish, first chill the gelatin mixture to the consistency of unbeaten egg white, otherwise the solids will either sink or float instead of remaining distributed throughout the dish.

to unmold: to loosen a gelatin dish from its mold quickly, hold the mold not quite to its surface in *very hot*—not just warm—water for about 15 seconds. Then cover with a dish and invert quickly.

TIP

- turn aspic or mousse out on a serving plate an hour or two before serving time, place in freezer for 15 minutes to reset any softening, and refrigerate until ready to serve. This saves time and trouble at the last minute.

AVOCADOS (alligator pears):

test for ripeness: use gentle pressure. A ripe avocado is soft-fleshed beneath its leathery skin. The skin should never be green if you are buying it for immediate eating; it should be well mottled with brown, or all brown. If you buy a firm green one, set it aside to ripen in a dark place for a couple of days.

to prevent discoloration: if you pull the skin off by hand you will not disturb the inner surface and it will retain its natural green color inside. If you do cut into the surface, rub with lemon juice and it will not darken.

to mash: press through a ricer for a fine uniform consistency.

B

BACON:

to store: bacon will usually freeze and keep well if stored in the tray just below the freezer of your refrigerator. Use the flat side of a table knife to separate the slices.

to dice: if you freeze bacon it will dice easily with a scissors or a sharp knife. Cut crosswise, close to the edge, across many slices at once. This will give nice thin uniform bits.

to cook: put bacon in a cold skillet, then heat with a low flame. This pulls out more fat. Pour fat off from time to time.

TIP

- if you have to make a lot of bacon at one time, try baking it. Spread on a rack over a shallow pan, place in a 350° to 400° oven, and cook until it reaches the degree of doneness you prefer. It is not necessary to turn it. Blot with paper towels when it is removed from oven. (Pour off the fat in the pan before you bake more.)

drippings: don't pour bacon drippings, or any other fat, down the drain; they will clog it eventually. Instead, keep a can beside the stove and empty drippings into this. When full, place can in the refrigerator until fat is firm, then discard with the garbage.

TIPS

- coffee cans with plastic covers are fine for this. Fasten the cover to the bottom of the can until the can is filled, then put the cover on the top, place in the refrigerator, as above, then discard. The plastic cover will prevent leakage in the garbage.
- to save drippings: if you save bacon drippings for cooking and flavoring, pour into small numbered or dated cans (frozen orange juice size is good) and store in the refrigera-

tor or freezer. Storage in large jars runs the risk of the bottom part becoming rancid before it gets used.

BAKING (see also CAKE):

temperature: test the accuracy of your oven heat gauge with a good oven thermometer. It may need adjusting by a stove man or handyman. You cannot bake or roast with predictability if your heat gauge is inaccurate.

cakes and pastries should generally be placed in the center of the oven for baking.

angel foods and sponge cakes should be baked on the lower rack of the oven.

BAKING POWDER:

to buy: baking powder loses potency when it stands long on the shelf. Buy small-size containers, unless you bake a lot.

substitution: if you find yourself without baking powder, 1 teaspoon baking soda and 2 teaspoons cream of tartar will replace 1 tablespoon of baking powder for most uses.

BAKING SODA:

use: to substitute sour milk, sour cream or buttermilk for sweet milk or cream in a recipe, add ½ teaspoon of baking soda for each cup of liquid. Sift the soda with the dry ingredients. If baking powder is called for in the recipe, deduct 1½ teaspoons of the baking powder.

Do not use soda in the cooking of vegetables. It has perfectly legitimate uses in cooking, but it is a great vitamin-C destroyer. It also imparts a slightly bitter taste to the vegetables. (If you want to keep peas green, see PEAS)

BATTER (see also CAKES, COOKIES, etc.):

to avoid lumps: use a wire whisk for stirring and beating.

to pour: thin batters, like those for pancakes or waffles, are best poured from a pitcher. It is easier to control the amount poured and there is less after-drip.

for a crisp crust: use olive oil instead of melted butter.

for a delicate crust: separate the eggs and add the beaten whites last, folding them into the batter just before using.

for coating meats, poultry or fish: add a tablespoon or two of sherry or brandy.

BEANS:

equivalents: one cup of small-size dried beans equals about 2½ cups cooked; of large size, about 2 cups cooked.

to shorten cooking time: soak dried beans in cold water for several hours; or cover with boiling water and let stand for an hour.

Lima beans:

to shell: with a scissors, cut a thin strip along the inner edge of the pod, where the beans are attached. They are then easily removed.

TIP

- put a whole onion in the pan in which you cook green Lima beans. This gives a nice flavor, and the beans need little else but salt and butter.

stringbeans: sauté stringbeans in a small amount of oil before adding liquid. This greatly improves the flavor and preserves vitamins, for it shortens the over-all cooking time.

TIP

- the fewer beans in the pan, the quicker they cook and the better they taste. If cooking more than 1 pound at a time, use separate pans.

BEEF (see also LIVER, MEATS, ROASTS, SOUP, STEWS, STOCK):

hamburger: (see MEATS, ground)

steak: for kinds of steaks, see "Definitions of Cooking and Menu Terms" at back of book.

General: the better quality steaks are not too lean; they should be at least slightly marbled with fat. The redder the meat, the fresher (less aged) the steak. A steak is more tender and flavorful when it is aged: slightly purplish in color, gives easily under finger pressure.

Thickness: a good thickness is 1½ inches. A steak should rarely be thinner than 1 inch.

To broil: (see also BROILING) thicker cuts of meat should be placed farther from the flame than thinner cuts, otherwise the center may remain raw. A very thick steak (2½ to 3 inches) may be broiled until well browned on both sides, then transferred to the oven to finish cooking.

TIP

- don't trim too much fat from a steak before broiling. It adds to the flavor and prevents drying. But remember to pour off the melted fat from time to time, to prevent its catching fire.

To time a steak: decide how thick you like your steak, and always buy the same thickness. Make a note of the length of time you must broil it to reach the degree of doneness you like; after an initial trial or two you need never over- or undercook a steak. Naturally you must always have the steak the same distance from the flame.

Test for doneness: a rare steak should test at about 130° on a meat thermometer, 140° for medium rare, 150° for well done.

or

- make a cut close to the bone or at the thick center of the steak and judge by the look.

or

- press down with 2 fingers. Rare steak feels soft, medium rare feels firm.

To turn a steak: use tongs rather than a fork, to keep the juices in.

To pan-broil: if your broiler gives you difficulties, don't hesitate to pan-broil a steak—it can be equally delicious. Pre-heat a heavy skillet which has been lightly but thoroughly wiped with fat or oil. Don't use any further fat. You can sprinkle the pan generously with salt instead, putting the steak in when the salt begins to turn dark.

TIP

- a small steak to be pan-broiled can go straight from the freezer into the pan. Use a low flame to start, and when both sides have been browned, use a cover to finish cooking. With proper timing, a small frozen steak will remain pleasingly rare inside, if you like them rare.

Swiss steak: the secret of excellent Swiss steak is to pound as much well-seasoned flour into it as it will take. Wait 20 minutes, then pound more in. Repeat this, if possible.

To tenderize a tough steak: you can't beat this old-fashioned method. Pound it with the edge of a small metal pie plate, or pot lid. (Flour can also be pounded into steak this way, as for braising.)

tongue:

Fresh: fresh beef tongue makes marvelous stew. Parboil it, then cut into pieces and treat like stewing beef.

Smoked: smoked tongue can be cooked quickly without lengthy prior soaking if you pressure-cook it 3 times for 20 minutes each, each time pouring off the water in which it was cooked and covering it with fresh cold water. Do not remove skin and roots until after the last cooking. You will have a very tender tongue, not too salty.

To peel: tongue should always be peeled while it is still hot. Do this under cold running water. It will be easier if you add a tablespoon of vinegar to the last cooking water.

BEETS:

to cook and peel: cook beets with skins on, then plunge them into cold water. Slip skins off with your fingers.

to have beets hold their color: leave skins on, as above, with about 2 inches of stem retained; a little vinegar or cream of tartar added to the cooking water also keeps them from fading.

young beets: young beets should be cooked with their greens attached. After cooking, slip off the skins but retain the greens, which are tender and delicious. (The greens can also be cooked and served separately, like spinach.)

stains: beet stains on plastic or wooden bowls are difficult or impossible to remove. Remember this when preparing or storing beets.

BERRIES:

to wash: if berries are well chilled before washing, they will be less likely to become mushy during the washing process.

BIRDS (see also CHICKEN, DUCK, TURKEY):

to truss: twist a pipe cleaner around the legs to hold them together while roasting. Spread the wings, then bend the second joint out and fold it under from the back; they will remain in place, without tying, close to the body. Large birds, requiring long roasting, should have the wings tied close to the body (use white string or dental floss) to keep the breast juicy; also tie the drumstick ends together.

stuffing: a stuffed bird must be roasted somewhat longer than an unstuffed one.

TIP

- if you plan to freeze a bird, cooked or uncooked, avoid stuffing it first; stuffing tends to draw out the moisture and juices.

To pack: if a stuffing contains bread or rice, pack loosely—these swell during roasting. If necessary, cook part of the stuffing in a separate pan.

To close: you may use the heel of a loaf of bread to hold the stuffing in, if the cavity opening is large. A stuffed bird can be easily and neatly closed if you use large stainless steel safety pins. Be sure they are stainless steel.

frozen birds: whole frozen birds should be thawed before cooking, otherwise the flesh tends to be stringy. Frozen parts such as legs, breasts, etc., can be sautéed without prior thawing, but these should be cooked under a cover for the early part of the cooking.

game birds:

To determine age: since only young game birds are tender enough for roasting (older ones should be stewed or braised) it is important to know their age. Look at the spur on the inside of the foot: an old bird is sharp-spurred, a young one has a rounded spur.

To cook: any game bird, cooked in almost any way, needs a liberal amount of added fat; wild fowl rarely lay on enough fat for essential flavor or self-basting during cooking. For roasting, tie strips of fat around bird or add fat to the pan, turning the bird often while basting. Wild fowl also need cooking at a higher heat than domestic fowl.

BISCUITS:

TIP

- biscuits will be crisp on the outside and flaky in the center if the dough is rolled thin and folded before cutting. They will also split open easily when you are ready to butter them.

BLENDER: when a recipe calls for forcing food through a sieve, try placing it in the blender instead.

TIP

- use the blender to purée any leftover vegetables, add gravy or stock: you suddenly have a fine soup!

BONITO: this is surprisingly like tuna fish. It comes canned—both flaked and solid pack, like tuna; and is much cheaper.

BOTTLES: use a nutcracker to open tightly screwed-on bottle tops.

BOUILLON:

to clarify: stir into the bouillon 1 egg white beaten with 2 teaspoons of water, plus an egg shell broken into small bits: this for each quart of bouillon. Boil for about 2 minutes, then strain through several thicknesses of cheesecloth draped over a large strainer.

uses: besides serving as a soup, use bouillon instead of water to add to gravies, cooking meats or vegetables; substitute bouillon for all or part of the water in cooking rice.

canned: canned bouillon or broth can be made completely free of fat if you refrigerate the can well before opening it, then pour through a strainer. (Keep a can or two of bouillon in your refrigerator regularly.)

cubes: avoid using more than 2 bouillon cubes in any dish—too many give a strong, unpalatable flavor.

BOUQUET GARNI: to make a herb bouquet which is easily removed from the cooking pot, wrap herbs (usually a sprig or two of thyme, marjoram, parsley and a bay leaf, fresh or dried) in a square gauze pad and tie with white thread. These pads are available at drugstores—size 3×3 is the most useful in the kitchen. Keep a box in your kitchen drawer.

TIP

- another method of enclosing a bouquet garni which is easily removable is to use an aluminum tea-holder, the kind that snaps shut.

BOWLS: substitute a large round plastic bowl for the usual heavy mixing bowl for cake batters, etc. A plastic bowl is much easier to lift for pouring and washing and is not so hard on the wrists, the housewife's favorite site for bursitis.

BRANDY:

to ignite: in making flambée dishes, you will have no trouble in getting brandy to ignite if you first heat the brandy gently, over a low flame. When it is quite warm, light a match, tilt the brandy slowly from the pan into the serving dish, and apply the lighted match to the fumes close to the surface of the brandy in the dish. It will ignite readily, in a running blue flame.

BRAZIL NUTS: there are about 40 nuts to the pound, unshelled, producing about 2 cups of coarsely chopped nutmeats.

to remove from shells: place nuts in a 400° oven for about 20 minutes. Remove, cool, crack lengthwise and shell.

BREAD (see also ROLLS):

to store: bread may be kept in the freezer, sliced or unsliced. Wrap as airtight as possible to prevent drying while frozen. Bread is generally easier to use if it is sliced before freezing and stored in a plastic bag. Frozen slices will thaw at room temperature in 15 minutes, or can go while frozen into the toaster.

TIP

- bread used within three days of purchase keeps best if wrapped in plastic and kept at room temperature. Ordinary refrigeration tends to dry out bread.

to reheat: when reheating bread in the oven, sprinkle it first lightly with water and place it in a brown paper bag. This will restore the fresh flavor without overcooking the crust.

For frozen bread: take an unsliced baked loaf straight from the freezer and place in a 400° oven for 15 to 20 minutes. The bread will taste like freshly baked bread, and will remain soft for about a day.

dough (see also FLOUR and YEAST):

TIPS

- a bit of sugar added to bread dough makes it rise more quickly. It also adds color to the crust.
- you can often do away with much kneading if you let your dough do its first rising in the refrigerator overnight. Cover with a dish towel.
- too much salt in bread dough will slow the rising action of the yeast.
- bread dough contains enough flour when it has become elastic and satiny upon kneading, with none sticking to your hands or to the kneading board.

- set yeast dough to rise in a warm place, about 80° to 85°. Don't set dough on a radiator top: this is usually too hot, and the temperature will kill the yeast. If you need some artificial heat, set the oven at very low, keep the door open and set the dough (covered) on a low stool near the oven door.
- yeast dough has risen enough if, after pressing the surface with your finger, a depression remains.
- yeast dough may be frozen, but the yeast is sometimes affected by freezing. It is better to make the bread or rolls and freeze them after baking. Also, frozen dough has a long way to go before it reaches the proper temperature for it to begin to rise.
- if your bread tastes "yeasty," the dough has probably fermented too long. Don't let it rise as long the next time, or else place the rising dough in a less warm place.
- make sure you use fresh yeast before going to the trouble of making bread. Otherwise the dough will not rise properly and your reward will be a heavy, graceless loaf.

Kneading: to knead bread dough, form it into a flattish ball, push the heel of your hand down into the center and push the dough forward and away from you. Then fold the dough back toward the center again, turn the ball slightly, and repeat. Occasionally turn the whole mound of dough over and do the same. If the dough remains sticky, sprinkle a little flour lightly over it while kneading. It is thoroughly kneaded when it is dry and satiny.

baking: in the oven, bread will rise higher and be lighter in texture if you do not light the flame until after you have placed the pans of dough inside.

TIPS

- bread made with milk instead of water has a more velvety texture; made with water, it has a crispy crust.
- to get a bread with a soft crust, brush it with melted fat several times during baking; or, during cooling, cover the bread well with a dish towel.

- to get a hard crust on bread or rolls, place a pan of boiling water on the floor of the oven during baking. Or bake at a slightly lower temperature.

Cooling: always remove bread promptly from the pan and let it cool on racks. Cooling in the pan causes the sides and bottom to become soggy.

crusts: save all bread trimmings and crusts from the making of sandwiches, etc., in a plastic bag, and store the bag in the freezer. When you accumulate enough of them use them for crumbs, bread pudding, stuffing or mix with ground meat for meat loaf.

stale bread:

Uses: make bread crumbs (see BREAD CRUMBS, below)

TIP

- stale bread can be used to prevent odor when cooking broccoli, cabbage, Brussels sprouts and other strong-flavored vegetables: put a couple of slices in the cooking water. Remove with a strainer by skimming.

BREAD CRUMBS:

to make fresh bread crumbs: remove the crusts of day-old white bread (set these crusts aside for future use, see above) and crumble the bread and rub through a coarse sieve.

TIP

- one slice of fresh bread equals ⅔ cup of soft crumbs.

to make dry bread crumbs: use either stale bread or white bread toasted lightly and allowed to dry at room temperature for a day. Place pieces of bread between folds of a dish towel and roll hard with a rolling pin; or place in a blender if you want them very fine. After pulverizing, you can complete thorough drying by placing the crumbs on a cookie sheet in a low oven without browning. Store in well-sealed jars. They will retain their flavor well for about 3 months.

TIPS

- you can add dried herbs and seasonings to these crumbs and thus have seasoned crumbs always ready at hand.
- one slice of toast equals ⅓ cup of fine crumbs.

to make buttered crumbs: toss soft bread crumbs in melted butter (about 1 tablespoon of butter to 1 cup of soft crumbs; or add 2 tablespoons melted butter to 1 cup dry crumbs).

bread crumbs as a thickener: dry bread crumbs are fine for creamed sauces to be used in casseroles or à la king dishes. Use wherever you like a toasted flavor in a sauce.

bread crumbs as a flour substitute in cakes: very fine bread crumbs can be used in place of part of the flour in many a cake recipe, particularly hearty cakes like applesauce cake or nut cake. Try this.

BROCCOLI:

to buy: look for bunches which are rich, dark green, with tightly closed buds. Over-age broccoli is lighter in color, the buds well opened, and may even show small yellow flowers. This is tougher, stronger in taste and has less flavor than young broccoli.

to prepare: soak in cold water to which some vinegar has been added, to rid it of insects. Rinse well.

to cook: if the stems are thick, slit them lengthwise halfway up or more. Cook, covered, in a heavy pan in salted water. (About 1 quart to a bunch of broccoli.) Lift the cover occasionally to keep the broccoli green. It will lose its color if it is overcooked.

TIP

- a couple of slices of stale bread in the cooking water will minimize odor. Skim the bread from the surface with a small strainer after broccoli is cooked.

BROILING (see also BEEF and FISH):

to avoid fat fires: when broiling fatty meats, drain off the fat occasionally to prevent its catching fire. If the fat does catch fire, clap a large pot lid down over it. If this does not smother the fire (it usually does) throw a handful of baking soda on it.

steaks, chops, etc.: make slashes, about an inch apart, on the fat surrounding steaks and chops, to keep the edges from curling.

TIP

- all meats should be turned only once. Cook the second side a slightly shorter time than the first.

to clean broilers: after meat is removed from the broiler, sprinkle the pan with salt or a detergent and cover with wet paper towels. This will make later cleaning easier.

a disposable broiler rack: line a cake or pie tin with aluminum foil, then stretch another piece of foil straight across the top, tucking the edges firmly around the rim. Make small holes in the stretched piece with a skewer, and broil on this surface. All the foil can be thrown away afterward.

rotisserie broiling: use only tender cuts of meat for this method of broiling (unless the meat has soaked in a tenderizing marinade). Center the meat on the spit to ensure proper balance. If broiling poultry, tie the bird compactly, with no wings or legs trailing.

To baste: if basting with a sauce, use the sauce only during the last half hour of rotisserie broiling, to avoid overbrowning.

BROWNING OF MEATS, CHICKEN, ETC.: make certain the meat is patted dry with a paper towel. Use a heavy pot, place meat in fat which has heated to bubbling; make certain the pieces do not touch one another.

or

(Chinese method) for quick browning, add a level teaspoon of sugar to hot fat, stir until it turns dark, and sear meat in this, turning frequently. You will get a beautiful mahogany color, with little sweetness discernible.

BROWN SUGAR (see SUGAR)

BRUSSELS SPROUTS:

to buy: pick tight, firm green sprouts. If the leaves are loose and pale, the sprouts are not fresh.

to prepare: wash well, then soak for 10 minutes in cold water with a little vinegar added, to draw out possible insects. Pull off loose leaves. Cut a little cross in the stem end.

to cook: parboil for 5 minutes and discard the water. Rinse, drain and cook again at a simmer for about 20 minutes—rarely more. A couple of slices of stale bread in the cooking water will minimize odor.

BURNED POTS: sprinkle the burned area liberally with baking soda, add only enough water to moisten well and let stand for several hours. You can generally lift the burned portion right out of the pot. A very badly burned pot may need two or more such treatments.

BURNS: every cook burns herself at some time. The pain will be less initially if you at once douse the burn with cold water. Brew some strong tea, cool it with an ice cube and brush it on the burn with your fingers. Repeat when it dries. Iced tea from the refrigerator will do fine.

BUTTER:

TIP

- it's a good idea to keep a can of butter on your pantry shelf for emergencies. Did you know you can buy canned butter? Gourmet shops stock it. It tastes very good, but it is expensive.

equivalents: one stick (¼ pound) equals 8 tablespoons, or ½ cup; ⅔ of a stick equals ⅓ cup; 5 and ⅓ tablespoons equals ⅓ cup.

to cut butter cleanly: either heat the knife blade or cover it with some clear plastic wrap.

in cooking: use sweet butter whenever possible. It is finer-flavored than salt butter. Since it does not keep as well as salt butter, stores stock less of it but buy it more frequently, so it is likely to be fresher when you buy it.

In sautéeing with butter, do not have the flame too high. Add the food as soon as the butter sizzles—butter browns and burns quickly. Stir or shake the pan often.

To serve melted or browned, be especially careful to heat butter slowly. Burned butter tastes bitter.

To clarify: heat butter gently only until it melts. Set it to one side of the stove until the clear liquid portion rises to the top. Skim this off carefully and use it for especially delicate butter sauces.

C

CABBAGE:

to cook: most people overcook cabbage. It should be slightly "crackly" to the teeth. Try slicing raw cabbage into thin strips first: it cooks in about 8 minutes. A couple of slices of stale bread in the cooking water will minimize odor.

To avoid "gassiness," give the cabbage an initial boiling for 5 minutes, rinse in cold water and cook again in fresh water to desired consistency.

red cabbage will hold its color if you add a tablespoon of vinegar or lemon juice, or ¼ cup of wine, to the cooking water.

in salad: blanch cabbage quickly, rinse in cold water, drain and refrigerate until ready to use.

CAKE:

baking: never try to bake cakes calling for low flat pans in high narrow ones. The batter will not bake through.

TIPS

- after greasing the pan, throw some flour on it and bang it about briskly until the sides and bottom are lightly coated. Empty excess flour from the pan and then pour your batter in. The cake will rise more evenly at the sides and will also be easier to remove from the pan.
- after the batter has been poured into the pan, tap the bottom sharply to release air bubbles.

chocolate cakes burn easily, so watch carefully while baking. You may have to turn the pan slightly every 15 minutes, or lower the flame after the first 15 minutes.

to test for doneness, insert a wire or thin skewer or a toothpick into the center of the cake. If it emerges clean and dry the cake is done.

cooling: allow cake to remain in the pan about 15 minutes after removal from the oven.

removal from pan: run a knife blade around sides of the pan, pushing against the pan rather than against the cake. Shake the pan lightly in an upward motion to loosen the bottom, place a plate or wire cake cooler over the top and invert quickly. Sometimes a few sharp taps on the bottom may be necessary.

If you still have trouble with cake removal, even though you have floured the greased pan, try this method: trace the outline of the pan on waxed paper, cut it out and place the waxed shape in the bottom of the pan. Grease the sides of the pan only. Pour in batter, bake, cool, run knife blade around sides and invert, as above. Remove waxed paper gently from bottom of the cake while the cake is still warm.

failures: if a cake is too coarse, the usual cause is under-mixing. Or perhaps you have used all-purpose flour when cake flour was called for.

- if a cake is too dry, this is usually due to too much flour in proportion to fat; or not enough liquid; or it was baked at too high a heat.
- if a cake has a hump in the middle, the oven may have been too hot. Too much flour will sometimes cause this.
- if a cake is higher on one side than on the other, your stove may need checking for proper leveling. Possibly the heat in your oven is unevenly distributed—this requires a professional stove man to correct.

TIP

- many cakes which for some reason seem to "hump" during baking will remain level if you cover the pan with aluminum foil during the first three-fourths of the baking period. Remove the foil for browning.

to ice a cake: (see also ICINGS) for a two-layer cake, place the bottom layer upside down and cover it with icing. Place second layer upon it, right side up. (To keep top layer in place, "pin" it with 3 or 4 toothpicks inserted here and there through the two layers, well spaced apart.) Ice the sides of the cake next; cover the top last.

ice cream cake: if your freezer is a very cold one, remove an ice cream cake to the refrigerator a half hour before serving, to make cutting and eating easier.

stale cake: don't throw it out—you can make a fine dessert with it. Soak pieces of stale cake in rum, then mix into a thick vanilla pudding and chill. Cover with whipped cream or decorate with split almonds or serve with fruit syrup. This becomes a company dish.

CAKE FLOUR (see FLOUR)

CANAPÉS (see HORS D'OEUVRES and SANDWICHES)

CANDLES: to make candles burn more slowly and last longer on your dinner table, place them in the freezer a day before you intend to use them.

CANS:

before use: always wash the tops of cans well before opening. Many stores spray their shelves with insecticides.

TIP

- if you shake most cans thoroughly before opening them, their contents will empty out cleanly with little need to pull them out with a fork or spoon.

can sizes: the most common can sizes, and their average contents, are:

8 oz.	1 cup
#300 (14½ oz.)	1¾ cups
#1	1¾ to 2 cups
#303 (16 oz.)	2 cups

#2 (20 oz.)	2½ cups
#2½	3½ cups
#3	4 cups

CANTALOUPES (see MELONS)

CARROTS:

to buy: for use as a vegetable course, buy young slender carrots. Older ones are thicker, tougher, sometimes deeper in color, and are best for soups and stews.

to cook: sliced lengthwise, carrots retain more food value than when cut in cross-section. Better still, cook young carrots whole.

to curl: cut the carrot down into several thin strips, to within half an inch of the small end. Soak in ice water until curled. Remove, drain and store in refrigerator until time to serve.

in salad: use a potato peeler to cut carrots into fine thin shavings and serve with greens in a tossed salad.

CASSEROLES:

to cook: most casseroles can be baked ahead of time until the last 20 minutes of cooking, then refrigerated; 40 minutes before serving put the oven at low (so that glass or ceramic dishes won't crack) and bake, gradually bringing the oven up to cooking temperature.

TIP

- if you are worried about a ceramic dish cracking, place it on a wooden board in the oven—a cheese-cutting board is fine.

to freeze: line your casserole dish with aluminum foil, then fill, cook and freeze. After the casserole is frozen remove it, foil and all, from its dish and store it in the freezer, well wrapped, thus freeing the dish itself for other uses.

dishes: baked clay (ceramic) or glass casserole dishes should never be placed over direct flame. Use an asbestos pad. If the clay is partially or wholly unglazed (rough, porous) don't soak it long in water, for unglazed clay absorbs water and may become useless.

CAULIFLOWER:

to buy: pick very white ones. A yellowed surface, or one covered with small gray specks, means it is not fresh.

to cook: if cooking whole, place the cauliflower in only enough water to reach but not cover the flowerets, for this portion cooks very quickly, and the steam will do the job.

TIP

- like cabbage, cauliflower need not be "gassy" if you first cook it for 5 minutes, rinse in cold water, and cook further in fresh water (as above) to taste.

To keep white: a slice of lemon peel added to the cooking water will help keep cauliflower white. So will ½ teaspoon of sugar.

To minimize cooking odors: add a couple of slices of stale bread to the cooking water. Scoop out with a strainer before removing the cauliflower.

CAVIAR: to use in canapés: when using caviar in any mixed dish, always add it just before serving, as the oil will smear or discolor the other ingredients.

CELERY:

to clean: use a potato peeler to rid celery stems of strings.

to cook: use a small amount of water and a low flame. Too fast boiling makes celery tough.

to crisp: let celery stand about a half hour in ice water. Or place in water in the refrigerator for 2 hours.

to curl: cut several long gashes in the stems down to about an inch of the end, then soak in ice water until it curls.

celery leaves: save these. Use them in soups, stews and salads. You can dry them (see HERBS) and use them as you do dried parsley and other herbs.

CEREALS:

to store: in most areas cereal products which come in boxes or bags (rice, flour, oats, grits, macaroni, etc.) can become infested with tiny crawling insects—these are weevils. To avoid infestation, keep all such foods in tightly closed jars, or place the package in a large plastic bag and twist the top closed with a rubber band.

to cook: add cereals slowly to rapidly boiling water so that the boiling point is not disturbed. This prevents gumminess. Be sure to use a large enough pot to allow for the rising of the sides without overflowing.

to use as crumbs: most dry cereals can be placed in the blender and pulverized. These crumbs are excellent in meat loaf, hamburger and for most of the purposes for which bread crumbs are used. (You can also make crumbs by rolling crisp cold cereals in a dish towel, using a rolling pin. To crisp the cereals, heat in a moderate oven.)

CHEESE (see also SOUFFLÉ):

TIPS

- cheese to be served at table should always be at room temperature. Remove it from the refrigerator well ahead of time.
- if you are not yet a cheese fancier, do not be deterred by the looks of some cheeses. Some cheeses taste their best when they look their worst. Experiment with different types. A rich realm of taste experience awaits you.

to store: the best wrapper for cheese, particularly the smellier varieties, is aluminum foil. Store in the refrigerator.

in cooking: no cheese should be cooked at a high temperature, for it becomes tough and stringy. A double boiler is the safest pot to use.

TIP

- a slice of Swiss cheese placed over many a cooked vegetable and heated until the cheese melts (or placed under the broiler until it browns lightly) makes a fine vegetable course.

to freeze: most cheese can be frozen and will keep well; upon thawing, they appear and taste much as they were before. This is true particularly of Swiss, and all the French, Italian and Greek natural cheeses; also cheddar. Process cheeses, however, do not take well to being frozen. For cottage cheese, see below.

grated: the two most common cheeses used for grating are Parmesan (mildly flavored) and Romano (sharp). But try also grating Swiss, Gruyère and cheddar for use on casseroles and vegetables.

TIPS

- keep a half-pound chunk of grating cheese wrapped in your refrigerator and grate it as you need it. It is more flavorful and much cheaper than ready-grated cheese. One pound of firm cheese equals 4 cups grated.
- if grated cheese is to be mixed into a hot dish, toss it in immediately before serving, otherwise it will become stringy.
- for use in soups, the ready-grated cheese you buy tends to make a soup cloudy. If you want melted cheese to float on top of a soup grate it freshly. Use Swiss, Parmesan, Romano, cheddar or Gruyère.

cottage cheese: this is a soft uncured cheese made from skimmed milk, sometimes called pot cheese.

You can freeze cottage cheese for later use in cooking. Freezing breaks down the curd and when it has thawed the cheese is easy to whip to creaminess. One pound cottage cheese equals 2 cups.

Creamed cottage cheese contains at least 4 per cent butterfat, to which salt has usually been added.

Farmer cheese is pressed cottage cheese made with some whole milk, thus has a somewhat higher fat content.

cream cheese: one pound cream cheese equals 2 cups. It can be frozen, with little change in texture upon thawing.

To spread: allow cheese to come to room temperature, then mix with a very small amount of any of the following: milk or buttermilk, sweet or sour cream, yogurt, onion juice, Worcestershire sauce, mayonnaise, soft butter, clam or vegetable juices.

Roquefort: to serve in cubes or squares, use a fork for cutting. The cheese then retains its natural crumbly texture.

CHESTNUTS: one pound shelled cooked chestnuts equals 1 cup puréed.

You can buy already shelled, dried chestnuts in Chinese or Italian food shops. Soak in warm water until softened, then drain and use in cooking or stuffing.

Roasted chestnuts have a nuttier flavor and are drier and creamier than boiled ones. But boiled chestnuts are easier to prepare.

to roast: for whole nutmeats: cut a cross in the rounded side of the shell with a sharp pointed knife and roast for 12 to 15 minutes in a pan containing 1 tablespoon oil, in a 450° oven. Shake the pan occasionally. Remove, and when cool enough to handle, peel. The inner skin usually comes off with the shell.

or

Place chestnuts in a slow oven and cook for 30 minutes. Open one. If it is soft and dry, the nuts are done. If not, continue heating them for another 10 minutes and test again. Be sure oven is not too hot or chestnuts will burst.

to boil: put nuts in cold water and bring to a boil. Boil for 30 minutes. Drain, place in cold water, and shell.

To make boiled chestnuts extra light: after boiled chestnuts have been removed from their shells boil them again for about 5 minutes, in milk.

CHICKEN (see also BIRDS):

to buy: try to buy fresh-killed (not cold storage) chickens; the latter are often chemically treated to slow down decomposition. You can be pretty sure a bird is fresh-killed if it has not been eviscerated before you buy it. If you live in a city, fresh-killed chickens are available at kosher meat markets.

To determine age (for frying or broiling, use only young chickens): A young chicken has a soft, flexible breastbone and is usually from 1½ to 3 pounds in weight. A medium-age chicken, from 3 to 4½ pounds, has a breastbone which is not yet rigid and skin which is still somewhat delicate—it should break without too much pull. Some of these can be fried, most are best for roasting. An old chicken has a rigid breastbone, is well over 4 pounds, is tough and dry-skinned and is lumpily fat around the tail. Such a chicken is good for stewing and soup-making.

to store: place an uncooked chicken in the refrigerator with no covering except a damp dish towel. Air must reach the bird or an unpleasant odor develops. Do not store more than 2 days.

to pluck pinfeathers: a tweezers or strawberry huller is good for this.

to eviscerate: the butcher generally does this for you when you purchase a chicken. If you do have occasion to do it yourself, make a slit at the tail of the bird, large enough for your hand to reach in comfortably. Pull out the organs gently but firmly, exerting pressure only where the tissues are attached to the inner wall of the body. You must take care not to break the gall sac (attached to the liver)—any part of the bird on which the dark yellow fluid falls is useless and must be discarded. Rinse the cavity well after removal of the innards.

to season: season all poultry the day before it is cooked, if possible. The meat is much more flavorful. But be sure to remove the bird from the refrigerator about an hour before cooking.

TIP

- one of the best herbs to use with chicken is tarragon. Soak a teaspoonful in half a cup of dry white wine for a half hour, pour the mixture over the chicken, then cook in any way you wish.

• see WINE for other tips on cooking chicken.

to broil: a very young chicken has little fat beneath the skin, thus the surface should be oiled or buttered before broiling.

Don't place chicken too close to the flame, otherwise the outside will char before the chicken is cooked inside.

to fry: chicken will remain tender and juicy if you follow these 3 frying tips:

(1) heat the fat well (but not to smoking) in a heavy frying pan before adding the chicken. There should be at least one inch of fat in the pan.

(2) turn the chicken once only.

(3) keep a lid on the pan until close to the end of cooking.

to sauté: use moderate heat—chicken sautéed in too hot fat has an unpleasant flavor. Cook skin-side down first, otherwise the skin will shrivel before it has cooked and browned.

Test for doneness: prick with a sharp-tined fork; if the juice which rises is clear and untinged with pink, the chicken is done.

to roast: a large chicken may be roasted breast side *down* for the first 40 minutes—this will keep the breast from drying out. Then turn chicken breast side up to complete the roasting.

To truss: twist a pipe cleaner around the legs to hold them together during roasting. Spread the wings, then bend the second joint out and fold it under from the back; the wings will remain in place, close to the body. A large bird requiring long roasting should have the wings tied close to the breast to keep the breast juicy (use white string). Also tie the ends of the drumsticks together.

Test for doneness: insert a skewer into the thickest part of the leg; if the juice which runs out is clear (not pink) it is done.

chicken livers: before using, examine each liver to make sure every part of the skin of the gall sac which adheres to the liver has been cut away. This skin is yellowish in color and will completely ruin the dish if it remains.

To cook: brown livers quickly at high heat for a short time, then cook gently at low heat, also for a short time. This ensures almost no loss of blood and keeps them tender.

chicken feet: ask your butcher for a couple of dozen chicken feet (he will probably not charge for them); have him chop off the nails. Feet are excellent for making chicken broth, stock or consommé. Scrub them, skin (see below) and cook until they fall apart, then strain and skim.

To skin: cook in boiling salted water until the skin loosens (about 5 minutes), then plunge in cold water and peel. (Chicken feet, cooked in the pressure cooker until the bones become soft and pulpy, make an excellent and inexpensive meal for a dog.)

chicken salad: chicken should be allowed to stand in its broth for an hour before being cut up. The texture and flavor are improved.

canned chicken: canned chicken is exceedingly soft. Don't expect to use a whole canned chicken in any intricate dish and have it hold its shape.

chicken croquettes: make these up well ahead of time and chill thoroughly. They are easier to handle when cold, and the taste is improved.

chicken broth: to give a gourmet touch to clear chicken broth, add a can or bottle of clam broth or clam juice to the hot kettle of soup.

CHILI SAUCE (see KETCHUP)

CHINESE FOODS: visit an Oriental food shop for some new food ideas: many kinds of noodles including shrimp noodles; bean curd (to serve in soup); fresh bean sprouts and bamboo shoots for mixed vegetable dishes and salads; ginger root for seasoning stews; fresh baby pea pods (snow peas) for stews; many kinds of dried beans; Japanese and Chinese mushrooms; plus many types of fish and meats, canned, dried and fresh.

CHIVES (see also HERBS):

to grow in the kitchen: buy a pot of chives, but transplant them to a larger pot with a drainage hole at the bottom, adding more soil. Water enough to keep the soil moist. They will grow for months if you place them in the light.

to cut: use small kitchen scissors to snip off chives as you need them for salads, soups or stews.

to freeze: wash the stems well, wrap while still wet in wax paper or plastic wrap, and place in freezer. Chives will retain their greenness if you use them as they are removed from the freezer, without defrosting.

CHOCOLATE (see also COCOA):

when melting chocolate to add to cake batter: add a little flour to the chocolate residue in the pan after the chocolate has been poured from it; mix thoroughly, then add to the batter. This removes almost all the chocolate from the pan.

for a quick icing: place a piece of sweet or semisweet chocolate on top of a hot cupcake; spread with a knife as it melts.

CHOPPING BLOCK: a wooden chopping block is extremely handy in the kitchen. You can buy one in practically any size, including the size of a small tabletop, or to fit over a piece of counter space. You will use it for everything from rolling dough to cutting up vegetables. Scrub daily and wipe dry. Once every 6 months cover it with vegetable oil and let stand overnight, then wipe off. At other times don't let water remain on it long. It will last indefinitely.

CINNAMON: mix your own sugar and cinnamon and keep the mixture in a jar (1 teaspoon cinnamon to 3 teaspoons sugar).

You can buy this mixture at about triple the price of making it yourself.

TIP

- put 2 or 3 sticks of cinnamon in a jar and cover them with sugar. Let stand for a few weeks. Use this sugar in your cakes for wonderful flavor. You may add vanilla pods to this also. Replace the sugar as you use it.

CLAM CHOWDER: if you use unshucked clams, scrub them well with a brush under cold running water and drop them, a few at a time, into ¼ potful of boiling water. Remove with a slotted spoon or small strainer as soon as they open (a couple of minutes), remove the clams and set aside, discarding the shells. Allow the broth in the pot to settle and pour off carefully, as there will be sand at the bottom. Use this broth toward the liquid of your chowder, adding the clams whole (if they are small) or minced, just before serving, to prevent their toughening. Very large chowder clams should have the tough muscle portions cut away, with just the soft "belly" used. A can of whole or minced clams added just before serving will give both richer flavor and very tender clams.

TIP

- if you are making New England clam chowder (with milk or cream and without tomatoes), be a purist: don't substitute bacon for salt pork.

CLAMS: different types of clams come from different waters. The hard-shelled chowders, cherrystones and littlenecks are all the same clam (Quohog) at different stages of development, the littlenecks being the youngest. There are also the soft-shelled clams (Ipswich) with long gray "necks," often called steamers. There are also razor clams, a great delicacy. These are the chief types from Eastern waters.

to test for freshness: a clam is alive, therefore fresh, if its shell is tightly closed. Never use an opened clam which will not close on handling.

to store whole, uncooked: clams can be stored in the refrigerator (on the lowest shelf) for as long as two weeks, provided you discard any which have opened. Keep them covered with a moist dish towel and examine daily. Naturally, the sooner they are used after you get them, the better they will taste.

to open: scrub clams thoroughly with a brush under cold water and let the clams stand out of water for 5 minutes or so until they are slightly relaxed. (When a clam is handled roughly it "clams up" and holds its shells so tightly closed that it is hard to wedge a knife between them.) With a little practice you will be able to tell that the clams are relaxed by the width of the crack between the shells. Pick up the clam lightly and place it in your left hand in the crotch between your thumb and index finger, crack side facing out. Take a short strong knife, place it quickly to the center of the crack (side of knife, not point) and push in *quickly,* using your right-hand index finger to give force to the thrust. Run the blade forcefully down and then along entire crack, cutting the muscle at the back which holds the shells together. If you are too slow with the thrust the clam will tighten again and you must set it aside to relax once more. This is not as hard as it sounds, nor is your leg being pulled. You can become an expert clam-opener in a very short time.

The lazy man's way to open clams: for serving clams on the half shell, this is really not so bad: it takes an expert to detect the difference. After scrubbing clams, drop them—about 4 at a time—in boiling water, allowing them to remain only about 15 seconds. Remove quickly with a slotted spoon or small strainer and open with a knife, as above. Refrigerate them on the half shell (see below). Dropping in boiling water for a few seconds relaxes the muscles just enough for you to slip the knife in easily. Beware of leaving them in the water placed in a plastic bag and rolled with a rolling pin to give

To store on the half shell: place clams in a flat pan or dish and cover well with clear plastic wrap, to keep them moist. Serve the same day as they are opened.

cooking: heat toughens clams quickly, so avoid overcooking.

to remove sand: clams from certain waters, or at particular times of the year, may contain a great deal of sand. They will discharge their sand if you cover them with a mixture of 1 gallon of water to ⅓ cup of salt, and let them stand about an hour.

or

The traditional method is to sprinkle the clams liberally with cornmeal, cover with fresh water, and allow them to stand about 3 hours.

COCKTAIL SAUCE FOR SHELLFISH: use some sherry in your mixture.

COCOA (see also CHOCOLATE):

to boil: boil cocoa in water alone for about 5 minutes before adding milk and sugar. This breaks down the starch and gives a more velvety texture.

to avoid skin: skin will not form on top of cocoa if you beat it until frothy as soon as it is made.

to substitute for chocolate: an equivalent for 1 ounce (1 square) of unsweetened chocolate is ¼ cup of cocoa plus 1 teaspoon of butter.

COFFEE:

to store: the flavor of ground coffee will keep better if the opened container is stored in the refrigerator. Cover it tightly, for it loses flavor when exposed to air due to the evaporation of volatile oils.

to make: there is no unanimity about how coffee should be made. Many experts feel that it is best made in a non-metal container and that the grounds should not be in too-long contact with the water. They favor the drip method, using an enamel or glass pot.

TIPS

- on the other hand, plain boiled coffee has its ardent proponents. There is no doubt that, when well made, it is excellent. Use plenty of coffee—to make it stronger, use more coffee per measure of water. Don't brew it longer than usual or it will be more bitter rather than stronger.
- *iced coffee tip:* pour freshly made coffee into an ice cube tray and let it freeze. Use these cubes to ice hot coffee whenever you wish it, without fear of diluting the coffee.

To make boiled coffee: for medium-strength brew, add 1 heaping tablespoonful of coffee to each measuring cup of cold water, set on the flame and allow it to boil at a rolling boil for about 1 minute. Remove pot from fire and when the coffee has quieted, sprinkle a few drops of cold water on the surface. This causes the coffee grounds to settle on the bottom. Then pour. For a stronger brew, add more coffee at the beginning of the process. This method makes really good coffee, and you need no fancy filters or coffeepots.

Instant coffee: if using instant coffee, you can get a more flavorful brew if you first pour the hot water in a pot, add the powdered coffee, and allow it to simmer for about 1 minute before pouring into cups. This tastes much better than adding boiling water to coffee powder in a cup.

iced instant coffee: you can make a quick (and pretty fair) iced coffee by pouring the desired amount of instant coffee powder into a glass, mixing with 1 tablespoon of boiling water, then adding ice water and ice cubes.

COLD FOODS: generally, dishes served cold need more seasoning than those served hot, as warmth releases the bouquet.

for picnics, school lunches, etc.: foods will keep cold longer if the insulated carrier in which they are to be packed is stored, open, in the freezer overnight. Then pack food in quickly and close the carrier. This also holds true for thermos bottles.

COLE SLAW: try preparing cabbage by putting it through the coarse or medium blade of the meat grinder. This saves time, and the cabbage does not crush.

CONFECTIONERS' SUGAR (see SUGAR)

COOKIES:

dough: the flour used in most cookie doughs is all-purpose rather than cake flour. Cake flour is too tender, unless a particular recipe calls for it.

TIP

- rolled cookie dough, like pie pastry, should not have too much handling, nor too much flour. Both of these toughen it.

To roll: if you roll cookie dough between sheets of waxed paper you will avoid the need to add more flour to the dough; it will also not stick to the rolling pin. This is easiest if the dough is chilled first.

To cut and shape: all cookie dough is handled more easily if it is chilled first.

TIPS

- dough will not stick to the cookie cutter if you dip the cutter in warm water between cookies.
- when using your hands to shape cookies, especially if the dough is rich, wet hands with cold water from time to time and the dough will not stick to your palms.

Refrigerator dough: this is handled most easily if it is stored in the freezer rather than the refrigerator. Then cut with a wet knife to avoid ragged edges.

cookie sheets: stainless steel cookie sheets are preferable to aluminum, since aluminum sheets eventually buckle and warp and give an uneven surface.

TIPS

- grease cookie sheets with either a solid vegetable shortening or with sweet butter (butter adds more flavor to the cookies). Don't use a liquid fat for greasing: the area between cookies will burn during baking, and this is very difficult to clean.
- if cookie dough has a large amount of shortening in it, it is not necessary to grease the pan. Most cookie doughs can be baked on ungreased pans.
- flour a cookie sheet after it is greased, and there will be less tendency for the cookies to thin out and spread during baking. A greased floured sheet is also preferred for any dough containing chocolate bits—the chocolate which comes in contact with the sheet is less likely to stick and burn while baking.

baking: rare is the oven which maintains a constant temperature throughout prolonged baking. If baking several batches of cookies, check the temperature from batch to batch—it may be necessary to set your oven regulator back; or else expect that the later batches will take less time to bake than the earlier ones.

Failures: cookies too crisp? You may have used too much sugar or too little fat in the dough. Try also closing them off from air when storing.

- cookies too soft? You may have used too much liquid or fat for the amount of flour. Cookies stored in airtight containers tend to remain soft; some become downright limp, such as soft ginger cookies. Many people prefer them this way.

to store: never store cookies in any container until they have thoroughly cooled.

TIP

- soft cookies, such as ginger cookies, should be separated from one another in the cookie jar by squares of waxed paper, otherwise they may stick to one another.

CORN:

to buy: never buy corn that has been husked. It has little flavor.

TIPS

- tear back the green husk a little bit to examine the teeth. Very dark yellow teeth indicate corn past its prime. Near-white teeth, very small, are too young to have developed much sugar yet. Try to pick corn which strikes a happy medium.
- if you have bought corn of doubtful sweetness, the best way to make the most of a bad bargain is to boil it in water to which sugar has been added: about half a cup to 2 quarts of water.

to remove the silk: if you have any trouble, use a rather stiff brush, such as a vegetable brush.

to cook: try roasting corn in your oven. Pull out the silk but leave the husks on. Roast at 325° for about 50 minutes. Remove husks (wear household gloves—they are hot!) and serve. This method gives much better flavor than boiling.

TIP

- if you boil corn, strip the ears, then make a layer on top of the water with the tenderer green husks, and boil. This adds to the flavor.

CORN BREAD: don't bake corn bread in too-thin pans or the outside will become overdone before the inside has baked.

CORNMEAL: as a coating or breading for fried, baked or broiled foods, cornmeal gives a tougher, coarser covering than crumb or flour coatings. This is fine for some foods—a cornmeal coating does have distinctive flavor—but for a thin, light crust use fine bread crumbs, flour or fine cracker meal.

CORNSTARCH (see THICKENING)

CORN SYRUP (see SYRUPS)

COTTAGE CHEESE (see CHEESE)

CRABMEAT:

to buy: crabmeat comes already cooked, packed in "lump" or in "flake" forms. The former is usually served for crabmeat cocktails, and is more expensive. Before buying, have your fishman empty the can in front of you: too often the top layer is "lump," but the portion beneath may or may not be. It is best to discover this at the fish market rather than in your kitchen.

Alaskan king crab, available both frozen and canned, is more like lobster in taste and texture than it is like ordinary (blue) crab.

to prepare: whether you buy canned or fresh crabmeat, finger through it carefully to remove the bits of shell which are always there.

TIP

- soak canned crabmeat for a short time in cold water to remove the "tinny" flavor which it sometimes has. Crabmeat thus rinsed is very much like fresh in taste.

CRABS: It is the meat of the blue crab which is sold cooked and packed in containers. The blue crab has a soft shell when it is caught in the spring or early summer, after it has shed its hard shell, but before the new one has grown. Clean soft shell and hard shell crabs in the same way (see below).

to clean (although this can be done for you at the fish market): wash crabs free of sand under cold water. With a small knife, remove the spongy substance under the side joints, and the pouch between the eyes. Or you can remove the entire head from just below the pouch.

CRACKERS: crackers of all kinds, plain or sweet, salted or seasoned in other ways, can be ground in a blender or placed in a plastic bag and rolled with a rolling pin to give crumbs for all sorts of uses, such as in meat loaf, meatballs or for a variety of toppings for baked vegetables, meat pies or puddings.

CRANBERRIES:

to store: whole fresh cranberries can be stored in the freezer in the same box in which you purchase them. Use them exactly as you would fresh ones, without defrosting.

TIP

- add a few cut cranberries to hot or cold sauerkraut.

CREAM:

sweet: when using cream in any dish cooked on top of the stove, avoid boiling, or it will curdle. Cook over a low flame, stirring constantly.

TIPS

- when you are not completely certain about the freshness of cream, beat in a pinch of baking soda. The cream will not curdle, even when added to hot coffee.
- for many cooking uses, undiluted evaporated milk can be substituted for light cream.

sour: any cooked dish containing sour cream will curdle if cooked at too high a temperature. When heating it, keep the flame low, or add a small amount of flour to the cream and mix well with a whisk while heating. If making a sauce, add sour cream at the end.

Substitutes: two fairly good substitutes for sour cream, if you need it in a hurry for a cooked dish:

(1) 2 cups buttermilk plus 3 tablespoons melted shortening, whipped well. This will give a good equivalent for 2 cups of sour cream.

(2) 1 can cold evaporated milk plus 1 tablespoon clear white vinegar, whipped well. This is a bit thin, unless the evaporated milk is chilled until ice crystals form, but it remains a good sour cream substitute for cooking uses.

whipped: cream doubles in volume when it is whipped.

Cream whips best if you do not whip too much at a time. A good rule of thumb is to see that the height of the cream to be whipped does not completely cover the blades.

To avoid spatter: find a high, narrow receptacle into which the beater blades will fit (a glazed ceramic flowerpot—without the hole, of course—is fine for this) instead of the traditional low round bowl. The cream also whips faster in a high narrow bowl.

For maximum frothiness: use day-old cream rather than fresh. Also, cream should be very cold; it is more likely to turn to butter during energetic whipping if it is warm.

If cream becomes buttery during whipping, add 2 tablespoons of cold milk and whip some more, carefully.

To prepare in advance: whipped cream will retain its lightness, height and texture for a day or more if you add 1 teaspoon of corn syrup to each ½ pint of whipping cream, then whip. This adds almost no perceptible sweetness to the taste.

To whip small amounts of cream: place cream in a cup or small bowl, use only 1 blade of the electric beater.

For guests: instead of serving plain cream with coffee, serve unsweetened whipped cream. A generous spoonful on each cup of coffee is a delightful Viennese custom.

CREAM CHEESE (see CHEESE)

CREAM PIES: cream pies, Napoleons, etc.—all desserts with custard fillings should be refrigerated at once and kept cold until serving time. Never allow them to stand for long at room temperature. Bacteria grow quickly in such a medium. Their refrigerator life is (safely) two days.

CREAM PUFFS:

to make: cream puff dough must be thoroughly beaten to give the puffs proper lightness and glossiness.

to bake: puffs must be baked in a pre-heated oven or they will not expand properly.

Tests for doneness: a properly baked cream puff is puffed and high, medium tan in color, and gives off a light papery sound when flicked with the fingernail.

Underbaking: a puff is probably underbaked if it shows beads of moisture. Return it to the hot oven, turn off heat, and leave for 5 minutes or so, keeping the door ajar.

TIP

- very large cream puffs may retain moist centers even when the outside has baked thoroughly. This may result in the puff's collapsing upon cooling. Remedy: slice off top of puff, remove all the moist dough with your fingers, then return the puff to the hot turned-off oven for 10 minutes, leaving the door ajar.

to serve: don't fill a cream puff until shortly before serving, otherwise it may become soggy.

CREPES:

to prepare: never overbeat crêpe batter—this toughens them. Let the batter stand for an hour in the refrigerator before cooking: this gives the crêpes a finer texture.

to cook: the chief trick, in achieving a successful crêpe, is to see that the bottom of the hot buttered pan is coated quickly with the batter, before it begins to set. Lift the pan from the flame for this. Very little batter is needed—only enough for one thin coating.

to flip: crêpes (and omelets) can be turned easily without using a spatula. Resign yourself to sacrificing several crêpes to learn this, and give yourself 20 minutes for practice. Prepare a small cast-iron omelet pan as recommended under OMELETS, make up your batter, cook one side as any crêpe recipe directs, and hold the pan over the kitchen sink for flipping. The secret is to flip it high—don't hold back. Anything that falls in the sink, forget. But 3 or 4 tries will have you catching the crêpe upside down in no time. Be brave! Flip it high! The knack stays with you forever.

CROQUETTES: mixtures for making croquettes should be very well chilled in order to make their shaping easier.

CUCUMBER:

to prepare: many cucumbers, these days, are sold with a paraffin-like coating to prevent deterioration. It is almost impossible to remove this—always peel them.

to slice: for a professional look to cucumber slices, score the cucumber from top to bottom all the way around with a sharp-tined fork. Then slice crosswise.

TIP

- a long thin slice of cucumber, when added to a punch bowl or mixed alcoholic drink (particularly those containing gin or rum) masks the alcohol taste surprisingly. Add several long slices to your next punch bowl.

CURRY: when making curries, the safest rule to follow is to use half the amount of curry powder or paste called for in the recipe, then add more to taste shortly before serving. (No two curry powders are the same strength, anyway.)

TIP

- add a teaspoonful of curry powder to biscuit dough, bread dough, dumplings, salad dressing, cottage cheese.

CUSTARD (see also CREAM PIES):

baked: for a rich brown crust, beat the eggs until frothy before adding them to the milk.

TIPS

- for a firm, smooth custard, beat the eggs only lightly. This will not give a brown crust, but it is fine for a custard which you wish to unmold.
- place custard cups in hot, not boiling water, when placing in the oven. Boiling water will cause the custards to become porous on the bottom and sides.

Test for doneness: insert the thin blade of a knife into a baked custard. If the blade comes out clean, the custard is done.

boiled: to prevent boiled custard from overcooking, remove the pan from the heat as soon as it is done, and place the pan in a larger pan of cold water.

TIP

- if custard begins to curdle due to excessive heat, pour it at once into a cold bowl and beat hard with a whisk.

Test for doneness: boiled custard is done when you have cooked it just to the point when the bubbles disappear. It is at this point when it should coat a metal spoon.

for pies: to avoid soggy pastry and to get a crisp undercrust: when making the custard, heat the milk to the boiling point before combining (slowly) with the beaten eggs.

D

DATES:

chopped: eight ounces pitted dates equal 1½ cups chopped. Chill dates in the freezer and you will find that cutting or chopping them will be easier. Also, dip knife or scissors in hot water now and then while cutting.

for use in cakes: toss chopped dates in flour before adding them to cake batter, and they will not sink to the bottom during baking.

DILL:

to use fresh: use scissors to cut feathery tips into cream sauces to be served with fish or vegetables; add also to leafy green salads for wonderful garden flavor.

to freeze: dill can be frozen in the same way as fresh chives (see CHIVES).

to dry: cut feathery fresh dill with scissors and allow to dry at room temperature for a couple of days, mixing it gently now and then to expose all of it to air. Then store in a tightly covered jar on the herb shelf. The flavor keeps very well for months.

use in pickling: do not buy young feathery dill for use in pickling brine. Ask for mature dill, or dill which has gone to seed. This is often sold dried and will do very well. Young dill such as that used for salads will not give pickles the proper flavor.

DISHWASHING:

for quick work: this is especially good if you have only a small space. It also uses less water: lather a sponge or dishcloth copiously and scrub rinsed-out glasses, silverware and dishes without running water, setting each to one side as soon as it has been soaped. Then rinse them, one after the other, under hot running water, and set to drain. This is *quick*.

Dishes or utensils which have contained eggs are easier to wash if cold water is used on them first, to prevent their coagulation and sticking to the dish.

for heavy pots and large platters: place a folded turkish towel or a small rubber sink liner across the top of one side of your sink. Rest heavy pots and platters on this when washing them.

DOUGH (see BREAD, COOKIES, PASTRY DOUGH)

DOUGHNUTS:

to prepare: allow doughnuts to stand for about 15 minutes after they have been formed, before frying them. They will absorb less fat.

when frying: turn doughnuts frequently and they will be less liable to crack.

To get a soft crust: dip doughnuts in boiling water as they come out of the frying fat. This also removes excess fat.

to sugar: shake doughnuts one at a time in a paper bag with a little confectioners' sugar.

DRIPPINGS (see BACON, *drippings*)

DUCK (for trussing and stuffing, see BIRDS):

to buy: a test for a young bird (the only kind worth roasting) is a soft flexible beak.

to roast: roast duck need not be greasy. Prick with a fork around the wings and the legs to allow the excess fat to run off during roasting.

to braise: prick as above, then sear the duck in a hot oven for about 20 minutes (releasing and discarding most of the fat) before cooking.

DUMPLINGS: dumpling dough will drop more readily from a spoon moistened occasionally in boiling water.

E

EGGPLANT:

to buy: the heavier eggplants are the better ones.

to peel: use a potato peeler.

to keep from discoloring: drop eggplant into salted water as you peel it.

EGGS (see also OMELETS):

TIPS

- there is no difference nutritionally between white and brown eggs.
- most recipes are constructed with medium eggs in mind.
- when serving egg dishes, use stainless steel flatware instead of silver; the sulphur in eggs discolors silver.
- some dishes call for egg whites only, others call for yolks. Make a list of recipes calling for each alone (see suggestions under *whites* and *yolks*) so you can use up whichever are left over.

to buy: look for eggs in cartons bearing the USDA (U. S. Department of Agriculture) seal. They are of better and more uniform quality. Look also for the date on an egg carton: choose eggs dated as close as possible to the day of purchase. Don't buy eggs over a week old. The date may be stamped on the carton (for example, Feb. 26 '68) or else it is coded by number ("57," meaning 57 days from January 1 equals February 26). The code number gets higher as the year progresses, but you can figure it out as above. It is a good idea to mark the current code number on your weekly shopping list.

to test for freshness: place eggs in cold water. Completely fresh eggs will lie flat on the bottom. Moderately fresh ones may have one end slightly raised.

TIPS

- if an egg rattles when shaken, it is not fresh.
- when opened, a fresh egg will show a thick white portion surrounding an upstanding yolk, with a more watery portion around the outsides. An egg with a flat yolk and a watery white is not fresh.

to store: don't wash eggs before storing them: the dull natural coating, the "bloom," helps protect their freshness. Store them with pointed ends down, preferably on a low shelf of the refrigerator.

to break: the yolk of an egg is less likely to break when the egg is cracked open if you hit the egg sharply but *obliquely* rather than straight across.

to clean up spilled raw egg: cover with salt, allow to set, then pick egg up with damp paper towels.

in cooking: when a recipe calls for many eggs, break each egg first into a saucer before adding it to the rest. A bad egg need not contaminate the others nor ruin a cake batter.

TIPS

- all egg dishes must be cooked at low or moderate heat, or they will become toughened.
- avoid beating eggs or egg yolks directly into any hot mixture. Either cool the mixture first, or add small amounts of the mixture successively to the eggs, beating well as you go. After several such additions, combine the two and beat again.

cracked: a few drops of lemon juice or vinegar added to the water often will prevent a cracked egg from breaking widely. Or wrap the cracked egg in aluminum foil before boiling. *Note:* do not use any egg which may have been cracked for some time, as it may harbor injurious bacteria.

boiled: remove eggs from the refrigerator a half hour before boiling, since very cold eggs may crack when placed in boiling water. If you forget to do so, run lukewarm water over the eggs before cooking; or add a teaspoon of vinegar to the water in which the egg is to be cooked; or puncture the rounded end of the egg with a pin before placing it in the water.

TIPS

- when it is important to boil an egg for a certain number of minutes only, place egg (at room temperature) in water which has reached the boiling point. Reduce heat to simmer and start counting the time.
- for soft or medium-soft boiled eggs, large or jumbo-sized eggs should be boiled about 1 minute longer than small ones.
- to distinguish between hard-boiled eggs and uncooked ones, spin them on their ends; an uncooked egg won't spin.
- you can hard-boil eggs so that the whites are firm but tender, and the yolks thoroughly cooked but still creamy: place eggs in a pot, cover with cool water and bring to a boil. Cover at once with a tight-fitting lid, turn off the flame and let stand 15 minutes. Eggs so cooked are ideal for stuffing, slicing or serving in any dish calling for hard-boiled eggs.
- for hard-boiling, eggs are less likely to crack if the water you start them in is at about the same temperature as the egg. Heat slowly.
- to avoid the greenish ring around the yolk of a hard-boiled egg, place the egg while still hot under cold running water and chill quickly. Eggs plunged into cool water are also easier to shell.

To peel a hard-boiled egg: it is very difficult to neatly peel an egg which is under three days old. For peeling whole, use slightly older eggs.

To slice hard-boiled eggs, dip the knife or egg-slicer in cold water, and the yolks will not crumble.

fried: eggs continue to cook after they have been removed from the pan, so fry or scramble them just short of the point you like before sliding them off onto a plate.

TIP

- if you like your fried eggs with the white coagulated but

the yolks still liquid, use a cover judiciously, lifting it often to see that you do not overcook. Or, when the yolk almost reaches the consistency you like, turn the egg over in the pan and immediately slide it onto the plate.

poached: to poach an egg when you have no poacher: boil water with a little vinegar or lemon juice added (to keep the whites from spreading), then turn down to simmer. Make a whirlpool with a spoon and open the egg into the center of the whirlpool. Gently and swiftly move the spoon around the edge of the pan, keeping the whirlpool going. Poach for 3 to 3½ minutes. Remove egg with a perforated spoon.

TIPS

- you can poach eggs in liquids other than water: tomato juice, soup or stock, beer, wine, milk. You can also serve the poached eggs with a sauce made from the thickened liquid, using butter and flour or cornstarch for thickening. Have the thickened butter ready while you are poaching the eggs.
- when using an egg poacher, always butter the rings before opening the eggs into them.

scrambled: for velvety, creamy eggs cook very slowly, starting with a cool buttered pan. Add a tablespoonful of cream or evaporated milk at the very end, stir in and serve.

or

Scramble eggs in a double boiler. They will remain moist, hot and creamy if kept in the top of a double boiler over hot (not boiling) water.

shirred: place a little butter on each yolk before placing eggs in the oven, to keep them from drying during cooking.

egg whites: make a list of recipes using egg whites so that you may use those left over from recipes calling for yolks alone. Some suggestions: meringue toppings for puddings; fruit whips; soufflés; white cakes; white icings; hard-boiled and finely chopped, then mixed with minced parsley as a garnish.

TIPS

- there are about 8 egg whites (from medium eggs) to a cup.
- egg whites can be frozen. Drop them into a glass or plastic container, allowing a little room for expansion as they freeze. Cover, and label the number of egg whites the jar contains. They will defrost at room temperature in about 2 hours, and can be used in the same way as fresh.

To whip: (see also MERINGUES) egg whites a few days old whip better than fresh ones.

TIPS

- egg whites at room temperature will whip to greater frothiness.
- *To whip 1 or 2 egg whites:* for small quantities, place whites in a cup or small bowl and use only 1 beater of your electric mixer.
- never add sugar to egg whites until the beaten whites stand up in peaks. Then add the sugar gradually, whipping well as you go. Sugar added too soon will produce a thin marshmallowy sauce which cannot be thickened.
- be sure that no yolk whatsoever gets into the whites, or they will not whip. To remove bits of yolk, use a large piece of eggshell.

egg yolks: make a list of recipes using egg yolks so that you may use those left over from dishes calling for whites alone. Some suggestions: hard-boiled and pushed through a strainer, for garnishes; added to cornstarch puddings (do not boil); sponge cakes; use in place of whole eggs in cakes (add a little milk for moisture); sauce thickeners.

TIP

- two egg yolks can generally be substituted for one whole egg in a cake recipe.

In cooking: for any sauce containing egg yolks, use a low flame or a double boiler, stirring constantly to prevent curdling.

TIP

- to blend yolks into a hot mixture, add successive small amounts of the hot liquid to the eggs, beating well each time. Then add this mixture to the hot one, stirring constantly; do not let it come to a boil. This will prevent curdling.

To hard-boil yolks separately from whites: separate the yolks from the whites, drop yolks into water which has reached the boiling point and been turned off (to keep yolk membrane from breaking). Then heat again very slowly and simmer for 8 minutes. Any white clinging to the yolk can be removed easily.

To store: there are two good methods for storing egg yolks in the refrigerator for near-future use:

(1) for use in cooking or salad dressing: beat the yolks and add ½ teaspoon cold water for each yolk. Store covered.

(2) for storing a raw yolk intact, without the membrane's breaking: first pour ⅓ cup of cold water into a small jar and dissolve ⅛ teaspoon of salt in it. Then gently slip in the whole yolk. The salted water should entirely cover the yolk. Drain carefully before using.

To freeze: beat egg yolks, mix with a little sugar or salt to prevent coagulation, then freeze, well covered. You can use these in most cooking which calls for egg yolks.

EGG WHITES (see EGGS)

EGG YOLKS (see EGGS)

ELECTRIC PERCOLATOR:

to clean: for a sweet, clean interior, fill percolator occasionally with hot soapy water plus 2 tablespoons of baking soda, and perk for 10 minutes. Drain, refill with hot water and perk 5 more minutes. Rinse.

ENAMELWARE: never use steel wool on enameled pots. If

any abrasive action is needed (but try soaking overnight with soap and water first) use a mild powdered cleanser like Bab-O and a sponge, or *lightly* use a plastic pot scraper, such as Tuffy or a Dobie pad.

ENGLISH MUFFINS:

to freeze: tear or slice muffins in half before freezing. Wrap them in plastic bags to prevent drying out. The frozen halves can go directly into the toaster.

TIP

- the frozen halves of English muffins will not stick to one another if you stack them with their cut surfaces *up,* one upon another.

F

FAT (see also BACON, *drippings*):

to remove from hot liquids: the best method is to pour the liquid into a jar or narrow bowl, allow it to cool, then refrigerate until the fat has hardened and can be removed with a knife or spoon.

TIPS

- a few raw lettuce leaves floated on top of soup will absorb fat quickly, and can be lifted out and discarded.
- wrap an ice cube in cheesecloth and run it quickly over the top of the hot fatty liquid several times. The fat will congeal and adhere to the cheesecloth.

to clarify: bring the fat to boiling, then strain through several thicknesses of cheesecloth draped over a sieve.

to discard: never pour fats down the kitchen drain. If it will congeal when cold, pour into a can and stand in refrigerator until it hardens. Discard with your garbage. If a liquid fat, flush down the toilet.

FIRE: if grease catches fire, immediately clamp a large pot lid down on it. Or pour baking soda on the flames and they will disappear.

Keep a small spray-type can of fire extinguisher within easy reach in your kitchen. Read the directions for use occasionally so that when you need it quickly you won't have to stop to read them.

FISH (for fish soups, see SOUP):

to buy: a fresh fish has glistening, protuberant eyes and a stiff —not limp—body. The flesh should spring back when pressed with the finger.

TIPS

- make certain the fish you choose has not been previously frozen; many frozen fish, fresh-looking in the showcase, tend to be poorly flavored. Buy fish in season, when you can get them fresh.

  Have your fishman leave on the top and bottom fins. These are attached to bones, and make removing the bones easier after the fish has been cooked.

to scale: always examine a fish for scales before cooking; few fish have had all their scales removed. Use a serrated grapefruit knife, hold fish by the tail on a flat surface and scale upward, toward the head.

to store: fish deteriorates rapidly, so should be used the day it is bought. If you must store it overnight, refrigerate it after having wrapped it well to keep the odor from permeating other foods.

frozen: use frozen fish immediately after thawing.

To thaw: if you must thaw frozen fish quickly, let it stand under cold (never warm) running water.

salted: salt cod, dried salt herring, finnan haddie, etc., should be soaked for 3 to 6 hours, depending on the fish, before cooking. And of course don't add salt to the dish.

TIP

- if you find salt fish too salty, try using milk in the cooking.

to cook:

TIPS

- lemon is the master of fish. Sprinkle fish liberally with lemon or lime juice and allow to stand in the refrigerator for about half an hour.
- remove fish from the refrigerator half an hour before cooking.
- fish are delicate-fleshed and dry out easily. Never overcook them.
- fish will have little odor in cooking if garlic, wine vinegar,

lemon or lime juice or white onions are included in the recipe.

- many an indifferent fish dish can be made into something special if you sprinkle it with grated cheese or cover it with a thin layer of Swiss, then place it under the broiler until browned.

Baking: fish will be less likely to dry out during baking if you lay a covering of oiled brown paper over them. Remove this toward the end of cooking if you want the fish browned or crisped on top.

TIP

- the best fish for baking are fatty ones like mackerel, tuna, whitefish, bluefish, shad, salmon and trout. The less fatty fish tend to dry out easily.

Broiling: make several light diagonal gashes through the skin, about every 2 inches, on both sides of the fish before placing it to broil. This helps keep the fish flat.

TIPS

- if using a grill, heat and oil it before placing the fish on it. Use 2 spatulas when turning, to avoid breaking the fish.
- fish fillets placed in a pan beneath the broiler flame need not be turned: the heat of the pan will cook the underside by the time the top is cooked. Be careful not to overcook.
- some cooks prefer to remove the skin from fish steaks before broiling them. Use a sharp pointed knife for this. This eliminates the fishy odor which some people find objectionable.

Frying and sautéeing: always pat fish thoroughly dry before dropping into hot fat, to avoid painful spattering.

TIP

- vegetable fats or oils do not absorb fish odor, thus can often be used again in cooking (after straining).

Tests for doneness: for deep-fat fried fish: the fish is done when it rises to the surface of the hot fat.

TIP

- for sautéed fish: use a toothpick to separate the flesh near the backbone. The fish is done when the flesh is no longer translucent.

Poaching: firm, smooth-fleshed fish are best for poaching: pompano, bass, striped bass, perch, red snapper, trout, salmon, halibut.

- the flesh of fish tends to break easily when simmered. Cook only until the white coagulates, then remove from the liquid carefully with a spatula. Or cook in cheesecloth, lifting out and unwrapping with care. This is best for large cuts of salmon, halibut, etc.

TIP

- any fish which has been poached or cooked in liquid and which is to be served cold should be allowed to cool in the liquid. It has more flavor and is also less likely to break on removal.

to remove fish odor and grease from cooking pan: pour half a cup of vinegar in the pan and boil. Then wash.

to remove fish odor from the hands: rub hands with salt, then wash; or wash hands in strong salt water.

to remove fish odor from the house: burn some sugar in a pan. The caramel odor seems to neutralize the odor of cooked fish. (You can use disposable aluminum-foil pans for this.)

FLOUR (see also SIFTING):

cake flour: cake flour is made of softer wheats than all-purpose flour, producing a delicate crumbly texture. The two flours cannot generally be substituted for one another in baking. *Note:* many boxed cake flours are self-rising (contain baking powder). Since most cake recipes don't call for self-rising flour, don't substitute this for the regular unless you delete the baking powder called for in the recipe.

bread flour (all-purpose flour) is a blend of hard and soft wheats and has a high gluten content which forms an elastic framework for holding the carbon dioxide bubbles released by the yeast. Breads should be made at least partly with gluten flour if you want them light.

TIPS

- often, when a recipe calls for sifted flour, you can eliminate the first sifting by deducting about 1 tablespoon of flour per cup when measuring, then sift (with other dry ingredients if called for) directly into the batter.
- there are new flours on the market which call for no sifting at all. These are fine for cakes, cookies, gravies, etc., but not so good for pastry dough, since the flour grains will not adhere to one another. For use in cakes, etc., use the same amounts as you would of regular sifted flour. They do save time and mess.
- keep a large shaker of flour (with good big holes) near your stove for dusting meats, fish, etc. You can also prepare it ready-mixed with paprika, salt, pepper, powdered garlic and herbs.

FLOUR SIFTER: don't wash sifter after each use. Bang it against a towel folded over the side of the sink.

FRANKFURTERS:

to avoid splitting during cooking: don't cook frankfurters at too high a temperature. Cook long and slowly. Don't prick them —they will lose some of their juiciness. Remove them with tongs.

FREEZER: wring a wet cloth well, wipe off the accumulated frost from your freezer shelves every few weeks. This will often do away with the need to defrost the freezer more than once or twice a year.

FREEZING FOODS: avoid seasoning food which is intended for freezing. Instead add seasonings during the later heating. Many seasonings lose their flavor when frozen.

TIPS

- foods placed in the freezer should always be wrapped as

airtight as possible, otherwise they will dry out and lose both texture and flavor.

- avoid freezing meats, fish or chicken when their surfaces are moist. Always pat them dry before wrapping them for the freezer.

FRITTERS:

batter: mix fritter batter only until just smooth, for a fine crisp crust. Overmixing causes toughness.

fillings: be sure the fruits, meats, fish, etc., used are thoroughly dried before being dipped in the batter, otherwise the batter will not adhere to them.

FROSTING (see ICING)

FRUIT CAKE: fruit cake may rise 2 or more inches during baking; remember this when pouring batter into the pan. To prevent a fruit cake from burning before the baking is completed, place a pan of hot water on the floor of the oven, replenishing it as necessary during the baking.

Here are 2 general rules for a successful fruit cake:

(1) the uncooked dough must be very stiff
(2) the cake must be baked in a very slow oven

FRUIT JUICES: save liquids drained from canned fruits and

(1) thicken them with a little cornstarch and heat, for use as a cake or pudding sauce
(2) substitute them for milk in cake batters
(3) freeze and save until you have enough to combine with gelatin for desserts and salads

FRUITS:

fresh: whenever possible, wash all fresh fruits with warm soapy water before eating; the skins have frequently been sprayed with insecticides before coming to market.

dried: dried fruits sold in bulk usually need at least an hour's soaking—or until they are plump—in cold water, before being cooked. Then take care not to overcook.

To chop: heat the knife with which you chop sticky fruits, like raisins and dates. Or use scissors, dipping them into water occasionally.

In batters: heat fruits (nuts too) in the oven before adding to cake or pudding batters and they will not sink.

or

Dust dried fruits lightly with flour before adding them to batters.

FRYING:

TIPS

- in any kind of frying, be sure the fat is well heated before adding the food, otherwise the food will absorb too much fat.
- any food to be fried must be thoroughly dried first; if necessary, pat dry with paper toweling.
- invert a colander or a large strainer over a frying pan whose contents spatter. Steam will be able to escape and you can avoid those small painful burns!
- don't cover foods which have been fried, otherwise their steam will make them lose their crispness. They will also become limp if placed on a cold dish—heat the serving plate first.

deep-fat frying: don't use butter for deep-fat frying; it burns quickly.

TIPS

- hot fat rises several inches when food is dropped into it. Choose a pot which will allow room for this.
- don't put too much food at one time in the hot fat, or you will lower the temperature of the fat, thus causing the food to absorb too much of it.
- be sure to keep the hot fat below the smoking point or you will get a bitter taste in the food, with lessened digestibility.

- always drain deep-fat fried foods well before serving them. Use crumpled paper towels rather than a flat absorbing surface, and much more fat will be absorbed from the food. You can also pat the top surface dry with another paper towel.

FUDGE: add a little corn syrup to the other ingredients when making fudge and the candy will be more creamy.

FUNNELS: keep funnels of different sizes in your kitchen, including one whose bottom opening is large enough to pour solid substances through, such as crumbs, flour, sugar.

G

GADGETS: avoid too many food-preparation gadgets in your kitchen. With proper use, a French chef's knife will take the place of many tools for mincing, slicing, chopping, etc. See KNIVES for how to use a French knife.

GARLIC:

to store: wrap garlic in wax paper and store in the vegetable bin of your refrigerator. It will keep for several weeks.

to mash: place garlic between 2 thicknesses of waxed paper and smash with a heavy knife handle. Slide the garlic off into the dish you are preparing and you will get none of the oils or juices on your fingers.

in salad dressings: when adding garlic to oil (or vinegar) for flavoring, impale each piece on a toothpick for easy removal.

Garlic oil: let garlic stand in oil a few hours or overnight, at room temperature—not in the refrigerator. This will extract maximum flavor.

Garlic vinegar: put several cloves of garlic in a bottle and cover with white or red wine vinegar. You can remove the garlic after a few weeks—you will have excellently flavored vinegar for use in dressings.

in cooking: when heated in oil, garlic browns and burns easily. Therefore do not have the oil too hot.

GARLIC BREAD: slice a bread partially through, spread it with melted butter in which garlic has lightly simmered, and place the bread in a brown paper bag and put in oven. The bag will keep the bread from becoming too crisp.

GARNISHES: to make a good dish look even better, don't neglect the little touches afforded by garnishes. Here are some ideas: parsley sprigs (or very finely chopped), watercress, fried or fresh onion rings (soak rings in salted water first to remove the sting), sliced gherkins, sliced stuffed or black olives, slices or halves of hard-cooked eggs, crumbled egg yolks, finely minced egg whites, fried toast points dusted with paprika, sautéed orange slices, diced cooked chestnuts. You can use small amounts of leftover vegetables, with or without mayonnaise or other dressings, arranged in interesting ways.

GELATIN (see ASPICS and GELATIN MIXTURES)

GINGER: one tablespoon of raw ginger equals ⅛ teaspoon powdered ginger, in flavoring power.

GLASS BAKING DISHES: remember not to set a hot glass dish on a very cold surface or in cold water—or vice versa, cold in hot—this will often cause it to crack.

GOOSE (see also DUCK):

to buy: a 10-pound goose will serve 6 to 8 people. Don't buy a goose which weighs under 8 pounds, as most of this weight will be bone.

to cook: a goose is very fat, so don't rub with oil or butter.

Goose is tougher than turkey or duck, therefore it should be cooked in a covered roaster except toward the very end, for browning.

GRAHAM CRACKER CRUST: if a graham cracker crust is to be used for a pie which has to bake, refrigerate the unbaked crust until it is very cold. Then pour in the filling and place the pie in the oven. This lessens the possibility of the crust's burning before the filling is baked. *Note:* don't use a glass pie pan when doing this, as it may crack in the hot oven.

GRAPEFRUIT:

to peel (see ORANGES, *to peel*)

to use skins as shells for salad, fruit cup, etc.: keep the grapefruit skins in cold water until serving time and they will be very firm.

juice: grapefruit juice can be used in place of vinegar in many oil-vinegar salad dressings.

GRAVY:

to thicken: for a clear gravy, potato starch, cornstarch or arrowroot are good thickeners; flour will make it opaque.

TIP

- if you use flour to thicken a gravy, try browning it first: put the required amount of flour in a frying pan over a moderate fire and stir constantly until it is the color of cinnamon. You will need no fat for this. Then add heated fat and warm liquid as you would ordinarily do. This gives a nice color and flavor to gravies. (This is the procedure used in making a brown roux.)

to avoid lumps: use a wire whisk for stirring and beating.

some tips for good gravies: never add liquid to meat before the meat has been seared and well browned.

- for a dark, full-bodied gravy, brown gently as much as 1 pound of sliced onions in a little fat; then brown the meat in this. Many onions are the secret of success.
- add 1 or 2 tablespoons of tomato paste to meat gravy. Also, half a cup of good red wine can do no harm; cook at least 20 minutes after adding these.

a non-fattening gravy base: for a thick, low-calorie gravy, boil many onions in a small amount of liquid until very tender, so that little or no draining is necessary. Then whip in a blender or force through a sieve. This purée can be flavored in any way you like for meats, fish, chicken or vegetables.

GRIDDLE:

to test for readiness to use: heat griddle, let a few drops of cold water fall on it. If the drops bounce and hiss, the griddle is hot enough to use.

GRIDDLE CAKES (see PANCAKES)

GUEST DINNERS: a trick one always discovers too late: write out your complete menu, down to the olives and relishes, and post it on that part of your kitchen wall (above the stove?) where it will stare you in the face during the last frantic minutes of preparation. Check it before bringing your guests to the table so that you will not forget to serve a single item you have prepared.

H

HAM:

boiled: to retain its juices, ham should be simmered, never boiled, for the required number of hours. For maximum juiciness, ham should be cooled in its own liquid.

baked: save the juices from sweet pickles or spiced fruits and use them to pour over ham slices to be baked in the oven.

fried: to fry thick ham slices, don't cook too fast. Turn several times to avoid burning and cook until evenly browned on both sides. They will remain tender and juicy.

ham and eggs: if you are a ham-and-eggs devotee, save some slices from your next baked ham (Virginia and Smithfield especially) to fry later with eggs. You can freeze these slices to use in the future. The conventional boiled ham slices which you buy are no substitute for the real thing.

HAMBURGERS (see MEATS, *ground*)

HASH: when making hash out of leftovers, remember that there should be about ⅓ as much gravy as the amount of solid ingredients.

HAZELNUTS: in culinary usage, cultivated hazelnuts are often called filberts. For improved flavor, toast them lightly in a 400° oven before use.

HERBS (see also CHIVES, PARSLEY, WATERCRESS):

TIPS

- use restraint when adding amounts and kinds of herbs to various dishes. You will soon determine the quantity and type you like in certain dishes—but begin by erring on the light side.

- avoid too many kinds of herbs in the same dish. Sometimes two and sometimes three may be used, but the combination should not overpower any one of them.

fresh herbs:

To grow: many herbs can be grown in pots near the kitchen window, or in window boxes. Plant seeds in the late winter or early spring and keep the soil moist.

To store: fresh herbs like dill, parsley, chives, basil, etc., can be kept in near-fresh condition if you wash them, shake them well, and place in tightly closed glass jars in the refrigerator.

To freeze: practically all fresh herbs can be frozen if wrapped airtight. The fresh green color will not disappear if you use them straight from the freezer, without thawing.

dried herbs:

TIPS

- dried herbs are more pungent than fresh, and should be used more sparingly.
- dried herbs rarely have a shelf life of more than three months. Open and sniff them occasionally, and replace them when necessary.
- always crush or crumble dried herbs well between the palms of your hands before adding them to your cooking. This releases the bouquet.

To make: place fresh herbs (celery leaves too) in a brown paper bag, twist it closed, and hang it up in your kitchen by a string. Shake the bag now and then, look into it in a couple of days. Drying time depends on the amount of moisture in the air.

To store: dried herbs keep best in opaque containers (to keep out the light) with screw tops or ground glass stoppers, away from heat. You can use ordinary glass jars if you cover the outsides with gummed plastic covering, like Contact.

herb butters: make up herb and other flavored butters and store them in small glasses in the coldest part of the refrigerator (you can freeze them too). You will always have these handy, and you might otherwise not take the trouble at cooking time to make these flavored butters, which make queenly dishes out of many plain-cooked vegetables.

HONEY:

to store: keep honey in a cool, dry place. Freezing will not harm it, although it hastens crystallization.

If honey crystallizes: stand the jar of honey in a pan of warm-to-hot water until it liquefies.

to pour: oil the inside of measuring cups or spoons before filling them with honey and the honey will pour out easily, leaving little residue. Wipe off the rim of the honey jar with a damp cloth before replacing the cover, and the cover will not stick.

HORS D'OEUVRES (see also SANDWICHES)

hot: most hot hors d'oeuvres can be made in advance, then refrigerated or frozen, then heated in the oven or broiler before serving.

TIP

- leftover meats, minced and mixed with pungent sauce, often make excellent hot hors d'oeuvres.

cold: make up and freeze small canapés. Remove them from the freezer about 2 hours before serving time. But don't freeze mayonnaise, as it darkens or separates. Don't use crackers—they get soggy.

TIP

- melba toast keeps its crispness better than crackers.

To store: cover tiny sandwiches with a thoroughly wrung-out damp dish towel, and keep in the refrigerator. Remove about 20 minutes before serving time so that any dampness will have time to disappear.

Cold canapé dippers: instead of the usual crackers, buy a can of tortillas. Cut the tortillas into quarters and sauté lightly until crisp. Drain and cool, and you will have delicious and unusual dippers to use in place of toast or crackers.

HOT LIQUIDS: run hot water first into any glass container into which you intend to pour hot liquid, to prevent cracking. If the container is small, place a metal spoon in it before pouring. The spoon carries much of the heat upward so that the glass will heat more gradually.

I

ICE CUBES: to get ice cubes clear and free of air bubbles, boil the water first to remove the air bubbles, pour into ice cube trays and cool, then freeze.

ICED COFFEE (see COFFEE, *iced*)

ICED TEA (see TEA, *iced*)

ICING:

to make: the chief secret of good icing is steady, constant and long beating.

TIPS

- when using confectioners' sugar, sift it first and you will have no trouble with lumps.
- don't add raisins or nuts to icings until the very last moment, otherwise the icing may stay thin.
- you can make chocolate icings with either baking chocolate or cocoa. For this purpose, ⅓ cup of cocoa plus 1 tablespoon melted butter can be substituted for 2 ounces of chocolate.
- a quick icing for cupcakes: place a piece of sweet or semi-sweet chocolate on top of the hot cake. Spread with a knife as it melts.

before icing a cake: cut triangles of waxed paper and arrange them, overlapping slightly, to form a circle on top of the plate. Place the cake on this. When you have finished icing it, pull the pieces of paper out, one by one, from under the cake. You will be left with a perfectly clean plate and a professional-looking job.

to spread: (see CAKES, *to ice a cake*)

TIPS

- icings will spread easily if you dip the knife blade in boiling water from time to time. This also gives a nice sheen to an icing.
- to ice a cupcake quickly, swirl it around, topside down, in the pan of icing, and lift it up with a flick of the wrist. It will look attractive. (Be sure all crumbs have been removed from the surface of the cake first.)

J

JARS:

to open: a hard-to-open jar will often open easily if you tap the cover, not too hard, flat down against the floor. This works better than tapping the side of the cover.

JELLY:

to make: fruit jellies and preserves always taste better when made in small amounts, so avoid doubling recipes.

TIPS

- if you want your jelly very clear, strain it several times through cloth.
- you can tell when jelly has boiled enough if it drops thick from a cold metal spoon, or if it jells on a cool plate. Remove the cooking jelly from the flame while testing.

To fill glasses: before pouring jelly into sterilized glasses, place the glasses in a pan containing a little boiling water to ensure that they do not break.

To seal glasses: before sealing jelly with melted paraffin, hang a piece of sterilized string over one edge of the glass. Then you will be able to lift off the paraffin easily.

JERUSALEM ARTICHOKES: these are not artichokes, nor do they come from Jerusalem. They are the tubers of a kind of sunflower and are delicious, with a nutty flavor.

to peel: to peel raw, use either a potato peeler or rub the skin off gently with a fine grater. If you cook them before peeling, peel them while hot; otherwise too much flesh will adhere to the skin. They are harder to peel when cooked, however.

K

KALE: this is cooked like spinach (see SPINACH, *to cook*), but takes a few minutes longer.

KETCHUP: once a ketchup bottle has been opened, refrigerate it. Otherwise both flavor and color deteriorate. This is also true of chili sauce.

KIDNEYS:

to remove membranes: use a nail scissors with curved blades.

to eliminate odor: first parboil kidneys in salted water, then discard the water and continue cooking further in whichever manner the kidneys are to be prepared.

KITCHEN LADDER: a low folding stepladder in the kitchen is just the right height to sit on, placing your feet on one of the steps, while washing dishes, peeling vegetables, mixing batters, ironing, etc. Sit down to do as much of your kitchen work as you can—you will be less tired at the end of the day.

KITCHEN TIMER: this is one of the handiest gadgets in the kitchen. Set it going, place it where you can hear it ring, and you need never forget you have something cooking.

KNEADING (see BREAD, *dough*)

KNIVES:

GENERAL TIPS

- always use the sharpest knives for food preparation. For general use, two important ones are a smallish finely toothed one and the large, heavy French chef's knife. You can almost make do with these two alone. A third good knife to have is the very long, very narrow type called a "steak knife."

to buy: buy good knives, they last almost forever. Stainless steel will not keep a sharp edge as long as do the old-fashioned carbon-steel types. Ask your butcher if you may not bring in your knives to be sharpened from time to time, when he sends his own out. He will probably charge you a small fee for this, but it is worth it.

how to use: for general cutting of foods, as a rule it is best to use a sawing motion.

How to use a French knife: for mincing, place the knife, sharp side down, and hold the tip to the cutting board with the left hand. Don't allow the tip to leave the board at any time. Do all the cutting at the broad end of the knife, near the handle. Use short up-and-down motions, moving the knife in a circle so that it traverses all of the food to be minced. Go back and forth, circular-wise, until the food is minced as finely as you like it. The same principle is used for slicing: remember to keep the tip of the knife on the board at all times.

to store knives: the safest and handiest place to keep your knives is on one or two magnetic knife-holders, placed high on the wall.

TIP

- steel knives which are prone to rust should be lightly wiped with vegetable oil before storing.

L

LABELS: form the habit of reading the weights and lists of ingredients on labels of bottled, boxed and canned foods which you contemplate buying. This will generally affect your buying habits for the better.

TIP

- make labels to attach to bottles and jars of the foods you store and freeze. A plastic adhesive tape will stick to glass or metal, can be written on and erased, and will withstand continued dishwashing.

LAMB (see also LIVER):

TIP

- lamb, properly, is meat from an animal which is under 1 year old. Older lamb is classified as mutton.

  "Spring lamb" comes from 3- to 5-month-old animals. This is now available all year round. "Baby lamb" is from an animal 6 to 8 weeks old.

chops: buy lamb chops at least 1 inch thick. Thinner ones will not be juicy and easily get overdone.

TIP

- the best chops for broiling are rib or loin chops. These are also the most expensive. Shoulder chops are cheaper, but generally tougher. (Cut up, they are excellent for stew.) A good shoulder chop for broiling, however, if you want to try a cheaper cut, is a round-bone shoulder chop. Ask for it by this name.

  Unless you are an out-and-out lover of well-done meats, broil or sauté lamb chops only until the centers are pink. The chop is juicier and tenderer and more flavorful.

roasts: do not remove the fell (the parchment-like covering) from a leg of lamb before roasting. It keeps the juices in and the roast will also cook more quickly.

TIPS

- squeeze the juice of an entire lemon over a leg of lamb and rub it well in before setting the meat in the oven. This tenderizes and adds greatly to the flavor.
- roast lamb served on the pink side (medium rare) is juicier and tastier than well-done lamb.

steaks: have your butcher cut a leg of lamb into thick steaks. They broil beautifully, are tender, will feed more people.

LEEKS: wash leeks very carefully under cold running water to remove the sand which is lodged between the flat leaves. Trim, and slice them lengthwise. If they are very thick, slice them in quarters lengthwise.

to cook: tie leeks in bunches and cook in boiling water until just tender.

TIPS

- substitute leeks for onions in soups and stews.
- serve cooked leeks just as you do asparagus, with your favorite sauce.

LEFTOVERS:

to store: label and pack away (airtight) leftovers in the freezer for future use. You may have ham today and ham tomorrow, but you needn't have ham again until next month, if you wish.

uses: many meat, vegetable and other food remnants can be cut into small pieces, mixed with beaten eggs, milk and a dash of imagination, then baked into a soufflé.

TIPS

- serve them up with an unusual sauce for an appetizer or hors d'oeuvres.
- put leftovers through a blender, or purée them, as a basis for a creamed soup.

- leftover cereal can be used as a thickener for stews, soups and gravies; it can also be combined with meats or vegetables in escalloped dishes.

Others: use leftovers in salmagundis, stuffed pancakes, omelets, fritters and croquettes, shirred eggs, stuffed vegetables, hash, sandwich spreads, spaghetti sauces, curries, minced and mixed with rice, as garnishes.

LEMON: lemon is said to be the master of fish. It can be extensively used also with meats and vegetables.

slices and wedges: lemon slices are hard to handle for use at the table. Serve them cut in lengthwise quarters or eighths.

TIP

- to prevent a lemon wedge from squirting in the wrong direction, prick the flesh first with a fork, then aim and squeeze gently.

juice: the juice of an average-size lemon equals about 2½ tablespoons, strained.

TIPS

- lemon juice is a fine tenderizer or marinade for meats. Rub the juice of an entire lemon all over a leg of lamb before roasting.
- if you need only a few drops of juice, prick one end of a lemon with a fork and squeeze out the required amount. The lemon won't dry out and can be kept refrigerated for future use.

but

- *To get juice from a dried lemon:* drop the lemon into boiling water and allow it to stand for 5 minutes removed from flame. Dry, then squeeze.
- to get the utmost juice from lemons, heat them in a 300° oven for 5 minutes. Remove, cool and store in the refrigerator. This increases the juice yield by at least one-third.

or

- Roll a lemon around on a hard surface, pressing with

the palm of the hand while doing so. This also releases more of the juice prior to squeezing.

If you use a great deal of lemon juice in your cooking, squeeze the juice of several lemons and store in a bottle in the refrigerator. The flavor lasts well for more than a week. Lemon juice can also be frozen.

Canned lemon juice: this does not taste as good as freshly squeezed lemon juice, of course. It can be used in cooking. But note that not all brands of canned or bottled lemon juice are freshly squeezed. Some are labeled "reconstituted." There is a difference in flavor.

grated rind: always scrub the outside of a lemon well with soap and water, dry, then grate. And grate only lightly so that you get only the yellow part—the white portion inside is bitter.

TIP

- the rind of an average-size lemon equals about 1 teaspoonful grated.

LETTUCE: there are many varieties of head lettuce on the market. Ask your vegetable man for Boston, Bibb or Butterhead—a tender change from the more familiar Iceberg or Simpson lettuce for your salads. Romaine is also a flavorful green; if the ribs seem too tough for salad, cut them out with two lengthwise slashes of each leaf and use only the leafy portion.

TIP

- don't discard the dark outside leaves of lettuce. Use them as greens in soups or stews.

to remove the leaves from a head of lettuce: core the solid part, the "heart," then hold the head upside down under cold running water. The force of the water will push the leaves apart.

LIMA BEANS (see BEANS)

LIMES: limes can be used in most of the ways lemons are used. They are also an excellent meat tenderizer: squeeze over meat and let stand half an hour before cooking.

LIVER:

to tenderize: for extra-tender steer, calf or pork liver, cover it with milk and allow liver to stand about 2 hours in the refrigerator. Dry thoroughly and dip in seasoned flour or bread crumbs for sautéeing or broiling.

to prepare: sliced liver to be sautéed or broiled should have the outer membrane removed first. This is easy: loosen a small portion of the membrane with the sharp tip of a knife, grasp with the fingers and pull off gently, all around the slice.

TIP

- lamb, mutton and pork liver should be scalded before cooking.

to cook: liver of any kind must never be overcooked, for it easily becomes tough. It should be browned quickly at high heat for a short time, then cooked gently at low heat, also for a short time. Turn once, but cook the second side still less.

to grind: it is not possible to grind raw liver without macerating it and causing it to lose its juices. Parboil or sauté it lightly first, then put it through the food grinder. Do not put it in the blender unless you wish a paste.

LOBSTER:

to buy: an uncooked lobster should always be alive, i.e., moving, when you buy it. It is darkish green in color. It becomes red when it is cooked.

Don't buy a cooked lobster if you wish to serve it in a hot dish. It will be tough, and often dry, if further cooking is required.

TIPS

- a live lobster may still not be a "fresh" one: it may have been kept for a week or more in a tank of seawater. The meat in such lobsters is puny. If you are in an area where lobsters are easily available, demand fresh-caught ones.

- if you buy a lobster already cooked, see that the tail is curled. This means that the lobster was alive (as it should have been) when it was boiled.

to boil: plunge live lobster, head down, into several quarts of salted water, with or without other seasonings, as your recipe may direct. Heat the water gradually to boiling and cook for about 25 minutes. (Scientists say a lobster feels no pain if the water is heated gradually; some people worry about this.)

- lobster toughens and shrinks from overcooking, so whatever your cooking method, be aware of this.

to eat: all parts of a lobster are edible but the intestinal vein which runs through the tail just under the back, and the "queen": a little bag near the head which contains gravel. The "coral" is the roe, and should never be discarded. It is delicious. The liver, called the "tomalley," is considered choice.

LOW SALT DIETS: foods containing little or no salt can be made more palatable by:

(1) judicious use of fruit juices such as pineapple, apricot, lemon, lime, etc., with vegetables and meats.

(2) adding liberal amounts of paprika to chicken, fish and meats.

(3) the addition of honey to many foods.

(4) caraway seeds and a pinch of sugar in spinach.

(5) adding a bit of sugar to the water in which fresh vegetables are cooked.

(6) the addition of nutmeg, as well as other spices and herbs. Make your own trials to taste.

When using salt substitutes, add them to the food just before serving. Cooking neutralizes their effect.

M

MACARONI: one cup of uncooked macaroni equals 2 cups cooked.

to cook: add 1 tablespoon of salad oil to the water in which macaroni is boiled, and it will be less likely to boil over.

MACKEREL (see also FISH): add some good dry red wine and a bay leaf when cooking mackerel, to remove the fatty taste.

MANGO

to buy: select mangos which are orange-yellow to red in color and which will give slightly upon pressure. Mangos bought too green may not ripen at home.

to ripen: slightly green mangos should be ripened in the dark, like tomatoes. Place them in a paper bag first. They are ripe when they develop a sweet fruity smell and become orange to red in color.

MAPLE SYRUP (see SYRUPS)

MARBLE SLAB: if you use a marble slab for rolling pastry (good, because the surface is always cool) never allow acid foods (vinegar, lemons, tomatoes, etc.) to come in contact with its surface: acid roughens marble.

MARINATING: a marinade should cover the food completely. You may use a dish as a weight, or a water-filled jar on top of a flat dish. Turn the food in the marinade occasionally. Or place the whole mixture in a large screw-top jar and invert it from time to time.

MARSHMALLOWS:

to cut: use scissors dipped in water.

MAYONNAISE:

to make: a proper mayonnaise made in your own kitchen is light, piquant in flavor, difficult to find as good in stores. Here are a few tips:

(1) be sure eggs and oil are at room temperature.

(2) use only fresh eggs and not too much salt. A little sugar helps to hold the emulsion.

(3) don't add oil too fast, or the mixture will not thicken. If you do make this error, place the container in the freezer for about an hour, take out and beat frenziedly (or put it in the blender) until thick, before adding more oil.

(4) use lemon or lime juice in place of vinegar for less pungency.

(5) add a few crushed mint leaves just before storing; or some minced watercress.

If mayonnaise curdles during the making, add a teaspoon of prepared mustard to a hot, dry bowl, then add 1 tablespoon of the curdled mayonnaise. Beat with a whisk until the mixture is smooth and thick. Continue, adding 1 teaspoon of mayonnaise at a time, beating well after each addition. The trick here is to add the curdled mayonnaise by single teaspoonfuls.

to store: mayonnaise may separate if it is kept too cold, so store it in the least cold section of the refrigerator (high up, or on a door shelf) where the temperature range is usually 55° to 68°.

If mayonnaise separates: sudden changes in temperature may cause separation. Beat briskly with a wire whisk, rotary beater or in a blender. A small amount of sweet cream may be added, with a pinch of sugar.

- any opened jar of mayonnaise, and all mayonnaise made at home, must be refrigerated.

to thin mayonnaise: if you find mayonnaise too thick for a particular use, try thinning it with sour cream.

in mixtures, canapé spreads, etc.: if you plan to store any mixture containing mayonnaise, omit the mayonnaise during the mixing, then cover the surface with it. Place in refrigerator. Just before serving, mix in the mayonnaise. This keeps the mixture from drying out or discoloring during storage.

freezing: mayonnaise can *not* be frozen. It separates.

MEASURING SPOONS: keep an inexpensive set of measuring spoons (held together by a ring) in every canister of flour, sugar, salt, etc., and replace them in the canister after each use. This is quick, handy and saves extra washing.

MEAT BASTER: you can buy a meat baster with a needle attachment, for injecting liquids—oil, wine, vinegar and spiced liquids of all sorts into roasts, turkeys, etc. This is a wonderful invention. A medical hypodermic syringe with a broad gauge needle will do as well.

MEAT GLAZE: this is a highly concentrated stock which is used in sauces, ragoûts, etc. To make a meat glaze, boil down 1 quart of rich stock to about 4 tablespoonfuls. Store in a small bottle in the refrigerator. It lasts indefinitely; a tiny bit goes a long way. Add a teaspoonful to an ordinary soup or gravy and it will no longer be ordinary.

MEAT GRINDER: to keep from slipping, place a piece of sandpaper, sand side down, on the surface on which the grinder stands.

MEATS (see also separate kinds of meat, as BEEF, PORK, etc. See also BROILING, ROASTING, etc.):

Note: the more exercise a muscle gets, the more flavorful it is. Since exercise tends to make muscle tough, the most flavorful cuts are generally those which require long cooking, such as pot roast, braises and stews. However, proper aging tenderizes meat, thus the loin—as in beef—can produce very flavorful and tender meat.

cuts (see DEFINITIONS OF COOKING AND MENU TERMS at back of book for names and descriptions of the chief cuts of meat.) Study the meat charts in your cookbook and learn from which part of the animal a particular cut comes. Every cook should learn to recognize a cut at sight. Your butcher will be glad to help you.

to store: Meats which deteriorate quickly must be used very shortly after they are bought: all ground meat (see *ground meat,* below), sweetbreads, tripe, brains, liver and kidneys.

Steaks and large cuts of meat can be stored two or three days in the refrigerator. Both flavor and tenderness will improve if you squeeze some lemon juice over it.

to prepare:

TIPS

- remove meats from refrigerator about 1 hour before cooking in any manner.
- for sukiyaki or any dish requiring very thin strips of raw meat, partially freeze the meat to make slicing easier.

to flavor: make up and keep, in a small jar, a combination of herbs, spices and other dry flavorings to add to meat loaves and stews, to rub into meats and chicken. This can rest at the side of your stove.

to cook: when a recipe calls for adding water to meat, substitute consommé, broth, stock, vegetable juices, wine, beer or diluted gravies.

ground meat: most dishes calling for ground or chopped meat such as meat balls, loaves, patties, etc., taste better if you use a combination of beef, pork and veal together. If you include pork, you must cook it thoroughly.

To store: any ground meat should be kept very cold and used as soon as possible, as it deteriorates rapidly.

TIP

- if you must store ground meat for a day or so in the refrigerator, flatten it out so that the cold can penetrate it quickly.

Meat loaf: when grinding crackers with meat for a meat loaf, add the crackers first and last to prevent the meat from sticking to the grinder.

TIPS

- a little cream, evaporated milk or vegetable juice mixed into a meat loaf will make it tenderer and juicier.
- cover the loaf with a light tomato sauce before baking and you will get a shiny, crisp crust.

hamburgers:

To buy: hamburgers and meat balls should not be made from very lean meat, for they will not have enough flavor and will dry out too easily.

TIP

- hamburger meat sold ready-ground at bargain prices is a doubtful bargain. It contains so much fat, usually, that it often shrinks to half its original quantity in cooking. A good cut for hamburger is lean chuck, ground to order.

To shape: shape hamburgers lightly, with little pressure; they will be juicier.

To cook: when broiling hamburgers, heat the broiling pan to very hot before placing the hamburgers on it; this will keep the juices in.

MEAT THERMOMETER: before inserting a glass-stemmed meat thermometer into meat, make a hole for it with a skewer, or the point may break. And always insert a thermometer through the fat side of the meat, being careful not to touch the bone. Bone conducts heat faster and you will get a false reading as to meat temperature.

MELONS:

tests for ripeness:

Cantaloupe (muskmelon): should have a shallow scar at the

stem end; it should yield to gentle pressure at this end. A ripe melon also has a sweet smell.

Casaba: a ripe Casaba is slightly springy when pressed lightly between the palms. Its skin color should be lemon-yellow.

Honeyball: same test as for Honeydew.

Honeydew: the skin should be creamy-colored and have a feel resembling soft smooth leather. The blossom end should respond to gentle pressure.

Spanish melon: this is difficult to test, for the melon has a hard rind which resists pressure. Look for a yellow (not white) underside.

Watermelon: shake it: a ripe watermelon has a slight rattle inside. Knock it with your knuckles: a ripe melon will give off a faint echo. If the sound is hard and dull, the watermelon is not ripe. Look at the stem end: the stem should be dark green, and the immediately surrounding area very dark green, almost black. A light green stem area suggests an unripe melon.

to chill: a properly chilled melon requires at least 1 full day of refrigeration before being served.

to store: cut melons absorb flavors from other foods in the refrigerator, so cover tightly.

MERINGUES (see also EGGS, *whites*)

to whip: there is almost no substitute for an electric mixer in order to avoid extreme fatigue.

TIPS

- egg whites for meringues should always be at room temperature.
- for an unsweetened meringue, add a pinch of baking soda to the whites before whipping. They will whip higher and be firmer.
- never add sugar to egg whites until they have been beaten until stiff enough to form peaks. Otherwise you will get a marshmallow-like sauce which will never become firm.

to spread: instead of smoothing a meringue over a pie, tart or cake, try spreading it roughly, making mounds and peaks. It browns attractively, looks more interesting.

to cut: for a soft meringue, cut with a buttered knife.

cause of "tears": if your baked meringue is covered with "tears" you have used too much sugar in the meringue; or you added the sugar to the beaten whites before they formed soft peaks; or the sugar was not sufficiently dissolved during the beating; or you cooled the pie in a draft.

meringue shells: you can practically always avoid failure if you have your oven *very* low, even at 200°, and you bake the meringue shells for an hour or more, depending on the thickness. Always grease the pan well, using a solid vegetable shortening.

Test for doneness: flick the shell with your finger—it should give forth a dry hollow sound. It is usually a pale tan in color.

MILK:

to store: milk can be frozen and stored in the freezer if it is in waxed containers or plastic cartons. Do not freeze in bottles. To defrost a frozen container of milk, let it stand in the refrigerator for a day and a half, or at room temperature from 4 to 6 hours.

to scald: rinse the pan first with water. This prevents the milk from scorching and sticking to the sides.

To prevent skin formation: skin will not form while you are heating milk if you cover the pan while it is heating; or beat the milk while it is heating.

in coffee: as a substitute for cream, milk will have a richer taste if it is scalded, then poured into the coffee while still hot.

to add to flour mixtures or mashed vegetables: warm the milk first. It has less tendency to cause lumps to form.

sour milk:

To make: add 2 teaspoons of lemon juice or white vinegar to milk (or cream) at room temperature, mix, and let stand for half an hour.

Uses: besides use in recipes calling for sour milk or buttermilk, sour milk can usually be substituted for sweet milk in cake or cookie batters if you add from ½ teaspoon to 1 teaspoon of baking soda to the dry ingredients. The resulting cakes and cookies are very tender.

buttermilk: this can be substituted for sour milk in any recipe.

To make: mix 1 cup of buttermilk with 3 cups of lukewarm skimmed milk (or skimmed milk powder mixed with water) and let stand at room temperature overnight, lightly covered. Mix and refrigerate. A portion of this buttermilk can be used in turn to make more.

evaporated milk:

To whip: pour the milk into a freezing tray and freeze it for about 20 minutes, or until particles of ice begin to form around the edges. Remove and whip briskly with a chilled rotary beater until thickened.

or

Heat milk in a double boiler over boiling water, just to the scalding point. Add gelatin which has been softened in cold water (1 cup evaporated milk calls for ½ teaspoon gelatin softened in 2 teaspoons of water); stir until dissolved. Pour into a bowl and chill, then beat with a cold beater until stiff.

To sour: for cooking and baking, a good sour milk can be made by mixing ½ cup of evaporated milk with ½ cup water; add 1 tablespoon of white vinegar and let stand for half an hour.

powdered milk: powdered milk mixes most easily if the water is at room temperature, or warmer. You can avoid lumps by beating briskly with a whisk, or pouring the water and milk powder into a screw-top jar, covering tightly and shaking vigorously. Most milk powders are of the instant variety and give little trouble in mixing, unless the water is ice cold.

To whip powdered milk: mix ½ cup milk powder with ½ cup

ice water and beat with a rotary beater until the mixture stands up in soft peaks—about 4 minutes. Then add 2 tablespoons lemon juice or white vinegar and beat until stiff. Fold in ¼ cup sugar. Serve at once. This makes from 2½ cups to 3 cups of "whipped cream."

skimmed milk: skimmed milk (or skimmed milk powder mixed with water according to directions on box) contains all of the nutrients of whole milk with the exception of fat and Vitamin D. It can be healthfully and economically drunk by overweight children and adults.

MOLASSES:

to pour: to aid in pouring molasses from a measuring cup, oil the inside of the cup first.

in cooking: to neutralize acidity, use ½ teaspoon of baking soda in any recipe calling for molasses.

MOLDED DISHES (see ASPICS and GELATIN MIXTURES)

MUFFINS: muffin batter should not be beaten too long, or the muffins will be coarse.

MUSHROOMS:

to store: wash mushrooms quickly, dry them, and place them in a plastic bag or container in the freezer, sliced or whole. Use without defrosting—they taste exactly like fresh mushrooms in any cooked dish.

TIP

- if a recipe calls for mushroom caps only, save and freeze the stems for later use in soups, stews, omelets or gravies.

to prepare: dark mushrooms, or those not in the pink of condition, should be peeled to make them look more appetizing. Firm white mushrooms need not be peeled; just wash them quickly, rubbing gently.

to keep from turning dark: white mushrooms will keep their color if you sprinkle them with lemon juice. Also, mushrooms will not turn dark if you steam them in milk or butter in the top of a double boiler for 20 minutes.

to cook: for a delicious low-calorie vegetable course, bake large whole mushroom caps for about half an hour, open side up, with nothing but a little salt added. Bake at about 300°. A pool of liquor forms in each cap, so don't fear that they'll dry out.

raw: very fine white mushrooms may be washed quickly and well, then sliced, and used raw in salads.

dried: there are many types of dried mushrooms available, all excellent for cooking and in soups and stews: the European variety, the Chinese (more meaty) and the Japanese (unusual; slightly crispy). Chinese and Japanese mushrooms require longer soaking (overnight) or cooking about half an hour at a simmer. Save the mushroom water for soup, gravies or in the cooking of vegetables.

MUSSELS:

to buy: like clams and oysters, choose only those mussels which are tightly closed. Discard all opened ones.

to clean: scrub mussels well with a stiff brush under cold water, then rinse well. (Wear rubber household gloves, since some of the shells may be sharp.) If the shells are very slimy, scrub with a little dry mustard first. Pull out the "beard."

to prepare: shake each mussel close to your ear; if it rattles or makes a slushy sound, examine it carefully: the chances are it may be filled with mud and small stones. One such mussel in a potful will ruin the sauce.

to cook: like clams and oysters, mussels toughen with overcooking. Cook in water or wine or other liquid at a gentle simmer only, and remove them the moment the shells open. Strain the liquid well to remove sand.

MUSTARD:

to make prepared mustard at home: mix dry powdered mustard with enough cool water to make a smooth paste. You may wish to add some other spices or flavorings. Allow to stand about 15 minutes before serving.

MUTTON (see also LAMB) mutton is hard to find in most American markets. Because of the low demand for it (and the high demand for lamb) it is rare and generally expensive. Mutton is tougher and has a more gamy flavor than lamb. Nevertheless it can be delicious. It needs to be cooked longer than lamb, and at a lower heat. It usually benefits from soaking—and tenderizing—in a marinade.

to prepare: mutton's strong flavor, which some people find objectionable, is mainly due to the outside fat. You may remove part of this before cooking. Or rub the meat well with lemon juice before cooking. You may also add lemon quarters to the water in which mutton is boiled.

N

NUTMEG: you can buy nutmeg already ground, of course, and it is flavorful; but it doesn't have quite the zing that freshly grated nutmeg has. Try buying them whole, and grate into your batter, atop creamed dishes, custards, etc.

TIP

- for use in cakes, it is handy to know that an average-size nutmeg equals about 2½ teaspoons grated.

NUTS (see also kinds of nuts, as CHESTNUTS, etc.):

to store: place opened cans or jars of nuts in the refrigerator. They will not become rancid as quickly as they will on a pantry shelf.

to blanch and skin: most nuts can be set to soak in boiling water until their skins wrinkle. With some, a quick rinse with cold water may follow this, but generally the skins will slip off easily.

to slice: nuts are more easily sliced and shredded if they are warm.

to grind: use a blender.

in batters: heat nuts in the oven before adding them to cake or pudding batters and they will not sink.

O

OIL:

in frying and sautéeing: add a tiny bit of butter or other solid fat to the oil: it browns the food nicely and adds flavor.

flavored oil: add a liberal pinch of any dried herb or combination of herbs and store for future use in salad dressings (straining off the herbs first). You can use garlic (see under GARLIC) for flavoring oils, or cloves. Experiment. You can then mix fine-flavored dressings in no time at all.

olive oil: the finest olive oil is a very pale yellow: this comes from the first pressing of the olives. It is more expensive than oil from the second and third pressings, which are progressively darker and greener in color—they are more heavy-flavored and not recommended for use in cooking unless you like a very strong olive flavor.

OLIVES (for Olive Oil, see OIL): the most common varieties of olives available in stores are the green Spanish olives packed in brine. Black (ripe) olives which come in cans are very tender and more delicate in flavor. There are also the Greek or Italian black olives, which have been marinated in flavored olive oil; some of these come partially dried and salted. If you are lucky, you can find green ripe olives, canned: these are meaty yet delicate, and are wonderful for marinating (soak for several days in a vinaigrette dressing).

OMELETS (see also EGGS):

omelet pan: you can use the traditional French tin-lined copper pan, but a small cast-iron skillet is excellent for omelet-making. To prepare one, fill it three-fourths full of vegetable oil and let it stand on a very low flame for 20 minutes; pour out the oil, wipe the pan well with paper toweling, and you have a pan which will turn out fine omelets if they are properly made. After each use, wipe the pan out well with paper toweling (and coarse salt, if abrasive action is needed) and hang it up for future use. Never use soap, since this removes the oils which have slightly seeped into the surface of the iron. A properly prepared pan will never cause an omelet to stick.

to prepare:

TIPS

- eggs for omelets should always be at room temperature.
- a proper omelet is best made with 3 eggs.
- for a delicate omelet, don't beat the eggs, just mix lightly only until the yolks and whites are combined.

to make: pour the lightly combined eggs into 1 teaspoon of butter which has reached the bubbling stage. It should be pale brown in color. Don't have the flame too low. When the eggs begin to congeal at the edges, draw them in toward the center with a fork, allowing the liquid egg to flow behind it. Continue around the pan in this way until the top is moist but not liquid. With a spatula, turn the omelet half toward the center of the pan, shaking the pan gently in that direction to help in turning. After only a moment slide the omelet off onto a warm plate. The center should be moist, and the whole very delicate.

TIP

- various fillings can be added before turning the omelet in the pan: sautéed mushrooms, onions, chopped meats and olives, creamed diced potatoes, etc. An excellent way to make use of leftovers.

ONIONS:

types: red or Italian onions are usually lighter-flavored and not as tear-inducing when you slice them, as the yellow-skinned. Italian onions are fine for serving raw in salads, on top of hamburgers, etc.

TIPS

- the very large Spanish (golden) onions are preferable in a dish calling for many onions: because of their size, there is less work in peeling and slicing. They are also sweeter, thus are fine for serving as a vegetable.
- white onions have the most delicate flavor, and are preferred for a dish like creamed onions. But these are more perishable than other types.

to peel: an onion is easily peeled while held under warm or hot running water.

TIPS

- cut a tiny slice from the top and the bottom end of an onion before peeling and the skin will come off more easily.
- if you are peeling an onion for the purpose of slicing it neatly, leave the "tail" (stem end) on, and it will give you something to hold on to when your knife gets close to the end.
- if you have many onions to peel, cover them with very hot water for a few minutes, then slip off the skins.

to chop, slice, etc.: see KNIVES, *how to use a French knife,* in order to chop, slice or mince onions in a trice.

To avoid tears: keep an onion or two in the refrigerator, replacing them as you use them. Slicing or chopping a cold onion causes almost no tearing. Refrigerated onions will keep fairly well if they are protected from outside moisture.

to store: for general storage, keep onions in a dry place, not too cold. Cut onions will keep for several days in the refrigerator if you place them in a screw-top jar (to keep the odor in). Don't store them in plastic containers—the odor will permeate the plastic.

TIP

- chop, then freeze onions in a plastic bag. They will keep

for months. Cook without defrosting, in any way you wish. This is a good thing to do with half a leftover onion.

in cooking:

General: most dishes calling for onions are improved if the onions are first sautéed lightly in oil or butter.

Sautéed: when sautéeing onions, use a cover for the first few minutes. This gets the onions tender before they begin to brown.

Boiled: cover very strong onions with boiling water, boil 2 minutes, drain, and cover again with boiling water to finish cooking. Some cooks do this a second time, using 3 waters in all. The resulting onions are very sweet and pleasant.

TIP

- boiled onions, if not cooked to mushiness, can be made firm (for stuffing) if you drop them gently into ice water as soon as they are cooked. It is important not to overcook these.

For a low-calorie sauce: boil onions until they are very soft, then press through a sieve or put in blender for an excellent and low-calorie sauce base.

onion rings: a shortcut to making french-fried onion rings: dip rings (well dried on paper towels) in pancake batter and fry quickly in hot fat.

or

Dust onion rings with flour before frying. This makes them crisp.

in salad: very strong onions to be served in salads can be "tamed" by soaking them, in rings, in cool water for an hour.

onion juice: sprinkle a little salt on the cut surface of an onion, then scrape with a knife or spoon to obtain the juice.

stains: don't leave brown or yellow onion skins standing for long in the sink: they stain some kinds of porcelain. (Household bleach usually removes such stains.)

to remove odor from hands: rub hands with either salt or vinegar, then wash with soap and water.

ORANGES:

to buy: thin-skinned oranges are generally the juiciest.

TIP

- it is more sensible to buy oranges by the pound than by the dozen, since the juicier the orange, the heavier. If you can only buy them by the dozen, compare relative values by weighing different-priced ones by threes.

to peel: thick-skinned oranges are easiest to peel, but the following method can be used for any orange: wash fruit, and cut off a slice of peel from the top and the bottom. Set orange, cut end down, on a cutting board and with a sharp knife cut off the peel in strips from top to bottom.

orange sections: to get clean orange sections devoid of the white membranes, first cover the unpeeled orange with boiling water and let it stand 5 minutes. Then peel.

grated rinds: save the rinds the next time you squeeze oranges for juice. Wash well, then dry in a very low oven or on a warm radiator top; grate and store in small jars. The grated rind, thoroughly dried, will keep for several months, ready for flavoring cakes, icings, custards, etc. You can also grate fresh rinds—allow the grated rind to dry out completely before storing.

- grate only the colored part of the skin, as the white portion is a little bitter.

orange juice: to give frozen orange juice a surprisingly fresh orange-juice flavor, add the juice of 2 fresh oranges to 1 can of frozen juice prepared as directed.

OVENS (see BAKING and ROASTING):

oven racks: if oven racks stick, clean them thoroughly, then coat the sliding portions lightly with petroleum jelly.

TEMPERATURES FOR ROASTING AND BAKING

	Minutes to leave in oven	*Fahrenheit*
beef roast, 3–4 lb., rare	20 per lb.	300
beef roast, 3–4 lb., well done	30 per lb.	325
rolls, yeast	15 to 25	400
biscuits, baking powder	10 to 15	425–450
cake, layer	25 to 30	375
cake, loaf	45 to 60	350
chicken, 4–5 lb.	1½ to 2 hrs.	350
fish, whole, 4 lb.	30 to 45	400
lamb, 3–4 lb.	35 per lb.	325
pie, filled, 2-crust	30 to 45	425
pie, shell only	8 to 10	450
pie, custard	15 at	450
	25 to 30 at	350
pork, fresh, 3–4 lb.	35 to 40 per lb.	350
potatoes, medium	50 to 60	400
turkey, 10–13 lb.	25 per lb.	325

OYSTER PLANT (Salsify):

to prevent its turning dark: drop peeled oyster plant in water containing a little vinegar or lemon juice. (Two tablespoons to a quart of water.)

OYSTERS:

to buy: buy and use only oysters with tightly closed shells. Oysters bought already shelled should be in clear, or only slightly cloudy, liquor; this shows that they have only recently been opened.

to open: use a beer can opener; insert the point under the hinge at the top of the oyster, and push down hard.

or

Set oysters in a moderate oven only long enough for the shells to open slightly. Remove and pry the shells open with a knife.

to cook: oysters toughen quickly and must not be overcooked. *To poach:* when cooking opened oysters in their liquor or in milk, cook only until the edges (gills) curl, or until the oysters are plump.

To fry: for frying, freshly opened oysters hold together better than those sold already opened, in containers. They also hold a crumb or cornmeal coating better when freshly opened.

TIP

- before frying (or broiling) oysters, it is best to remove the slippery coating by poaching them quickly (about 1 minute) in their own liquor. A crumb or batter coating adheres more easily to a poached oyster.

oyster stew: sprinkle a little nutmeg over a bowl of oyster stew before serving it.

P

PANCAKES:

batter: for very tender pancakes, prepare the batter the night before, omitting the baking powder. Add this in the morning, then cook.

TIPS

- for high, light pancakes, use sour milk or buttermilk instead of sweet milk, adding a pinch of baking soda to the batter. Or see recipes for buttermilk pancakes.
- the less liquid you use, the heavier and more dense the pancakes will be.
- add a finely chopped banana to pancake batter. Or almost any minced food—an epicurean way to use leftovers.

griddle: between batches, rub the hot griddle with salt tied in a piece of gauze. This removes bits of cooked batter and results in less sticking.

to cook: use about ¼ cup of batter for each pancake.

- never turn a pancake back on a side which has already been cooked; this toughens it.

to keep warm: place pancakes in a low oven, between folds of a dish towel to keep them from becoming soggy.

to store: make and freeze pancakes, separating them with squares of waxed paper. To serve, place them frozen under the broiler or in a 375° oven.

PAPAYA:

test for ripeness: papayas are ripe for eating when the skin is a deep yellow or orange and the flesh is slightly soft to pressure.

PAPRIKA:

to buy: try to get real Hungarian paprika—it is more full-flavored than ordinary paprika.

uses: use plenty of paprika when making pot roasts; it not only adds marvelously to the taste, it gives a beautifully colored gravy.

- you can use paprika with a large number of chicken, meat or fish recipes, as well as sprinkled over many vegetables. Use it in soups and stews, and with rice.

PARSLEY (see also HERBS):

to store:

In refrigerator: wash, then place parsley in a covered jar in the refrigerator. Parsley will keep well for over a week.

In freezer: wash, remove stems and place the leaf heads in a covered jar or plastic container in the freezer. The color and flavor keep excellently.

To dry: place parsley in a brown paper bag and hang it somewhere in your kitchen by a string. Shake the bag once a day: drying time depends on the amount of moisture in the air. You can also dry parsley in a low (200°) oven, stirring or shaking now and then. Or dry in a tray on top of the radiator. When thoroughly dried, place in airtight bottles away from light and heat.

to chop finely: dry parsley thoroughly with a dish towel before cutting, otherwise the pieces will stick together and not disperse into fine flakes. (See KNIVES, *how to use a French knife,* for this purpose.)

If frozen, rub the parsley leaf heads vigorously between your palms and they will crush into fairly fine flakes.

PARSNIPS: tender and sweet, parsnips should be served as a vegetable in their own right, rather than only as a component of stews or soups. You can treat them as you do carrots, except that they require shorter cooking time.

PASTRY DOUGH (see also PIES):

TIPS

- avoid overmixing pastry dough; throw it together only long enough for it to adhere roughly into a ball.
- lard makes pastry dough very tender and light in color; a little butter adds flavor. If you use vegetable fat instead of lard, try a touch of butter to this also.
- chilled dough handles more easily than dough at room temperature, so refrigerate it before rolling.
- contrary to the old precepts, it is not necessary for anything but the water to be iced when putting together a pastry dough. But once the ice water has been added, avoid too much handling.

for a flaky pastry: measure the flour and fat and refrigerate both in the bowl for at least an hour before you start mixing. (Then use ice water, naturally.)

for a tender crust: add half the shortening to the flour first, then cut to the consistency of cornmeal. Add the rest of the shortening and cut quickly to the size of small beans. Then add ice water and mix.

for a crust which will not absorb moisture (good for juicy fruit pies): this is also nice and flaky: substitute an egg yolk for 2 tablespoons of the water in the dough. Mix the yolk with the remaining water and let it chill before using.

to store pastry dough: wrap the dough well in plastic covering and refrigerate. It will keep well for 3 days. Or line a pie tin, wrap well in plastic covering, and freeze. It will keep for months.

frozen pie crusts: always let a frozen crust thaw, unwrapped, before baking, otherwise the inner surface may remain raw and moist.

- if you freeze an unbaked pie crust in a Pyrex pan, you must let the pan come close to room temperature before filling and baking, otherwise the pan may crack in a hot oven.

PEACHES:

to peel: very firm peaches can be peeled with a potato peeler. Or let peaches stand for about 3 minutes in water which has been brought to boiling and then turned off. Drain, peel peaches with a firm downward pull.

PEANUT BUTTER:

to store: most types of peanut butter are homogenized; still, in some the oil has a tendency to rise to the top. Store jar upside down on your shelf.

PEAS:

to keep their color in cooking: fresh peas will keep their green color in cooking (providing you don't overcook them) if you raise the lid occasionally. Never cook them to softness—they should be a tiny bit crisp for maximum deliciousness. Never use baking soda—this will keep them green, but it gives a slightly unpleasant taste.

frozen: peas can often be separated from one another while in the frozen package if you hit the package hard on all its sides and corners before opening.

PECANS:

to remove nut meats whole: cover nuts with boiling water and allow them to stand until cold. Then crack end-to-end in a nutcracker.

PEELING VEGETABLES: peel potatoes, onions, carrots, etc., over a newspaper, then throw out all the waste at once, with no messiness or cleaning-up necessary.

TIP

- a potato peeler is useful for many other vegetables: carrots, turnips, parsnips, heavy-skinned squash, eggplant. It also does a great job of clearing celery totally of strings.

PEPPERS: green or sweet red peppers do not keep well. Use them shortly after they are bought, refrigerating for a couple of days if necessary.

PICKLES: when making pickles, use plain (not iodized) salt, or you will get an unpleasant flavor. Coarse salt is preferable to table salt. For some reason, it gives a better flavor to pickles.

PIES (see also PASTRY DOUGH):

pie tins: pies are best baked in tins from which the outside shininess has worn off. A completely new tin tends to overcook the bottom. If you are starting with new ones, try using a screening bottom first.

French tart tins are pie tins with removable sides. They come in many sizes, and are desirable if you wish to remove an entire pie without damaging the side crust. To remove, place the tin on an inverted bowl whose diameter is a little smaller than the tart pan. Loosen the side spring and push down gently to release the pie.

for a pie with a glossy top: brush the top crust with milk before baking.

to get top crust to stick to bottom crust: moisten the rim of the bottom crust, place top crust on and pinch the edges together all around the rim.

to bake a pie shell without its buckling: fill unbaked shell ⅔ full with small dried beans, then bake. Or prick unbaked shell all over with a fork, then bake. The first method is preferable.

juicy pies:

To avoid a soggy bottom crust: line pan with pastry dough, then brush bottom and sides with beaten egg white, allowing to dry before filling.

or

Sprinkle fine bread crumbs lightly over the bottom crust before adding a juicy filling; this will keep the filling from remaining loose, and will also prevent sogginess of the bottom crust.

To prevent boiling over: push a few pieces of raw macaroni through the top crust before placing the pie in the oven. These will allow steam to escape. Or prick over the top crust well with a fork before baking. The first is preferable, since the juices will not rise and disfigure the looks of the top crust.

- *if* juices do boil over onto the oven floor, sprinkle salt over them to prevent smoking.

PINEAPPLE:

test for ripeness: pull out one of the inner leaves of the crown. If it comes out easily, the pineapple is ripe.

to store: cut pineapple should be kept well-covered in the refrigerator, since butter and milk absorb its odor easily.

PLASTIC DISHES:

to remove stains: tea, coffee and juice stains can be removed from most plasticware by soaking with a solution of laundry bleach and water. Stubborn stains will require a stronger solution. Rinse well.

POACHING (see EGGS, FISH, etc.): poaching usually requires very little liquid, enough to barely cover the food; and should be cooked at a simmer.

POPCORN: to make popcorn pop like mad, pour kernels into a strainer, wash in cold water, drain well, and pour into the popper.

TIP

- for an interesting and delicate flavor, add half a peeled garlic clove to the melted salted butter which you use on popcorn.

POPOVERS:

TIPS

- iron muffin pans produce the best popovers.
- pour popover batter into hot muffin pans rather than cold ones, and they will be lighter.
- popovers always double in size when baked. Allow for this expansion when pouring batter—a shade less than three-quarters full is safe.

Test for doneness: a popover is done when it has "popped" and slips easily out of the pan.

to store: popovers can be put in the freezer for future use. When wanted, put them—still frozen—in a brown paper bag, in a 425° oven for about 5 minutes.

PORK (see also LIVER, MEATS):

to cook: always cook pork until it has lost its pink color. A meat thermometer is the most reliable guide for knowing when the proper inner temperature—about 190°—has been reached. Never eat pink pork.

ground: a butcher is not allowed to grind raw pork in the same machine in which he grinds other meats; unless he has a separate grinder for pork alone or unless you buy your pork at a "pork store," you must grind pork in your own food grinder. Be sure to scrub the grinder afterward thoroughly, with a brush and scalding suds. Boil it for greater safety.

chops: pork chops should be about 1 inch thick. Thinner ones tend to dry out during the prolonged cooking which pork demands.

Test for doneness: prick chops with a sharp-tined fork: if the juice which rises is clear and untinged with pink, the chops are done.

POTATO CHIPS: for an interesting garlic flavor, let a peeled clove of garlic stand in the container with potato chips for a few hours.

POTATOES:

TIPS

- avoid stirring or pushing potatoes about with an implement while cooking: they crush and break easily. You need generally only shake the pan briskly from different directions. If necessary, lift and turn them gently with a spatula.
- to keep their color: raw potatoes will not discolor if you immerse them in water before you peel them. Or rub oil on your palms and roll each well-dried potato in your hands so that a thin covering of oil adheres to their surfaces.

baked: the best potatoes for baking are Idaho potatoes, which have an interesting mealiness. If you use new potatoes, since they contain more moisture than old ones, they require longer baking time.

For mealy, dry potatoes: prick potatoes with a fork before baking.

For a soft skin: rub potatoes well with fat before baking.

To shorten baking time: run a long heavy nail lengthwise through each potato and leave in during baking. The nail carries the heat to the center.

To avoid sogginess: if you have not pierced the potato skin before baking, do so immediately upon removal from the oven: this allows the steam to escape.

boiled: put a piece of bacon or smoky sausage in the water in which you boil potatoes, for flavor.

To peel boiled potatoes: potatoes boiled with their skins on are easily peeled while they are still hot. If you have boiled potatoes for cold potato salad, don't wait for them to cool before you peel them.

mashed: potatoes intended for mashing must not be boiled too long or they become waterlogged. They are ready for mashing if they break apart when pierced with a fork.

Before mashing, drain potatoes well and place in a pot over a flame, shaking until they are dry. Then mash.

To make mashed potatoes white: after cooking potatoes dry, mash and beat them with a little scalded milk.

For fluffiness: add a bit of baking powder toward the end of mashing. Whip well with a whisk or fork.

TIP

- you can mash potatoes ahead of time and reheat them, but brush the surface with a little melted butter when they are first made, to prevent a crust forming.

french-fried (see also FRYING, *deep fat*) don't prepare french-fried potatoes until just before serving, otherwise they are likely to become soggy.

TIPS

- dry potato lengths quickly and lightly with a dish towel before dropping them into deep fat and you will be less likely to lower the temperature of the fat. You will also avoid painful spattering.
- don't put too many pieces of potato into the frying basket at one time; too many lower the fat temperature so that the potatoes, in order to become thoroughly cooked, will absorb and retain too much grease.

escalloped: to prevent milk from curdling when baking escalloped potatoes without flour, first add only half the milk called for and bake in a low to moderate oven. Add the remaining milk gradually during the baking period.

TIP

- never fill the baking pan more than three-quarters full before setting in the oven, otherwise it will boil over.

with roasts: bake potatoes in the same pan with roasting meat so they will absorb its flavor; but wait to place them until about 40 minutes before the roast is done, otherwise they will fall apart.

TIP

- potatoes cooked with roasts need not always be skinned first. Scrub them well, dry, rub with a small amount of fat between the palms, and place as above. They are also more nutritious this way.

potato salad: don't use baking (Idaho) potatoes for salad; they are too mealy, and break easily.

TIP

- mix the dressing with the potatoes while they are still warm; this allows the potatoes to absorb the flavors. Also, serve freshly made potato salad while it is still warm, instead of the traditional cold salad. It is much more delicious.

grated: when grating potatoes for potato pancakes, etc., sprinkle lemon juice over the top and cover, to keep the grated potatoes from turning dark.

As a thickener: grate raw potatoes into clear soup and simmer for a minute.

POTATO PEELER: use a potato peeler for peeling cucumbers, eggplant, squash, carrots, apples, firm peaches, celery, turnips, parsnips, pumpkin.

POT LIDS: remove the lid from any cooking pot by opening out, away from you, to avoid a sudden burst of steam in your face.

POT ROAST: always sear meat first, in a small amount of fat or oil, over a high flame. Turn it until all sides are well browned. This seals in the juices and guarantees good flavor.

cooking liquid: try substituting beer for water or stock in a pot roast. About ½ a can, mixed with some tomato purée, will give a magnificent gravy.

POTS AND PANS (see also OMELETS for omelet pans): for most cooking, heavy metal pots and pans are best, either cast iron or enamel on iron. They distribute the heat well, will not dent as easily as thinner metal and are less likely to scorch food. But get in the habit of using two hands to lift them, to avoid future trouble with your wrists!

TIPS

- food chemists say that cooking foods in cast-iron pots or pans adds valuable iron to the diet.
- unless you intend to boil liquid in it, grease or oil the inside of any pan, enamel-covered as well as metal. Use a folded paper towel for this. Whether you intend to sauté, stew or braise, foods will be less likely to stick to an oiled pan or pot. This is also a good practice when using Teflon-coated pans (see below).

to measure for size: measure across the tops of pans, not the bottoms.

Teflon-lined pans: pans of all varieties are now on the market which are lined with Teflon or a similar plastic substance enabling you to fry or sauté foods without added fat. This is possible because such a lining makes use of whatever fat is in the food itself: an egg, for example, contains a small amount of fat (in the yolk); meat, chicken and fish likewise contain enough fat in themselves to sauté successfully in such pans. Thus anyone wishing to limit his fat intake would be wise to buy one or more of such pans. *But note:* foods which contain practically no fat (onions, for instance) will not have a sautéed flavor, although they will cook without sticking. For such foods use a tiny amount of fat or oil, or merely lightly grease the pan.

To buy: try to find steel or club aluminum or (for baking) glass pans lined with this coating. Ordinary aluminum buckles in time. Unfortunately most of the Teflon-lined pans on the market seem to be the latter.

To reheat foods: Teflon-lined pans are admirable for this. Cooked rice, for example, may be reheated as is (covered, and stirred from time to time), and should not stick or burn if you use a moderate flame and are alert.

To wash: use a sponge or a cloth with soap and water—never any abrasive. But the metal underside of the pan may be scoured with steel wool like any other pan.

POULTRY (see BIRDS, CHICKEN)

PRESERVATIVES: there is some difference of opinion with regard to the safety or desirability of using preservatives in canned, bottled or boxed foods. There is no reason why you should not play it safe and try, whenever possible, to choose those prepared foods which do not have preservatives or additives in the contents. Read labels carefully.

PRESSURE COOKER: a pressure cooker is invaluable for the quick cooking of tough meats. Read directions in the booklet which accompanies the cooker—you need very little water when cooking in these, but you do have to pay strict attention to the time. (See TONGUE)

to open: never try to remove the lid before the pressure has completely subsided. Run cold water over the closed pot to bring this about quickly.

PRUNES: for a richer syrup when cooking prunes, use prune juice in place of some of the water. Also, try using honey in place of sugar. And a few thin slices of lemon are not amiss here.

PUDDING:

packaged pudding: two good ways to avoid lumps when mixing pudding powders with milk:

(1) pour milk into a large screw-top jar, add the powder, screw top tightly and shake briskly. Pour into saucepan and cook.

(2) use a wire whisk—you can do the mixing in the saucepan. But always add the powder to the milk, not vice versa.

Puddings for children and invalids: any packaged pudding which requires cooking can be made more nutritious if you add an egg or 2 egg yolks, and an extra ⅓ cup of milk to the usual recipe. Follow cooking directions, but keep just below boiling.

saucepans for puddings: don't cook puddings in too-thin pots, or the bottom is very likely to burn.

to keep a skin from forming: lay a piece of wax paper directly on the surface of a cornstarch pudding when it has been poured, and leave until it cools.

to unmold: most cornstarch puddings will unmold when cold if you run a knife blade around the inside of the mold and invert; if you are in doubt, oil the mold lightly before pouring.

pudding sauce: a good quick sauce to serve over a dessert pudding or plain cake: cook a package of vanilla pudding according to directions, add 2 tablespoons of rum, and cook again until slightly thickened. Pour while hot.

R

RADISH ROSES:

to make: cut the peel down from the top in narrow slices almost —but not quite—to the bottom of the radish. Place them in ice water and they will open.

RECIPES: always assemble all ingredients of a recipe before getting to work. This saves time and footwork, and also enables you to discover when you are out of something before you are halfway through your preparations.

REFRIGERATOR DOUGH (see COOKIES)

RICE:

TIPS

- 1 cup uncooked white rice equals about 3 cups cooked. 1 cup uncooked brown rice equals about 2½ cups cooked.
- long-grain rice is nice in appearance, also more expensive than short-grain. But for croquettes, puddings, etc., the short-grain is more sensible.
- if you are in a city where you can buy imported Italian rice (it's expensive) try it once: it is unusually delicious —has a waxy-surfaced quality which keeps the grains separated and has an excellent texture.

to cook:

To avoid sogginess: don't add cold water or other cold liquids to hot rice. Keep some simmering beside your cooking pot if necessary to add more liquid during cooking of rice.

TIP

- rice cooks better in low, wide pans than in high narrow ones.

For better flavor: use liquid other than water in cooking rice: bouillon, stock, vegetable juices, etc.

For light fluffy rice: wash uncooked rice thoroughly, perhaps 3 times, to remove excess starch before cooking.

To make cooked rice whiter: add 1 teaspoon of lemon juice to the water in which you cook rice.

The absorption method: many chefs prefer this method of cooking rice: place washed rice in a low pan with a tight, heavy cover and add double the amount of boiling liquid. Cover at once and set over very low flame until all the liquid has been absorbed. The rice may be tossed lightly with a little melted butter before serving.

or

Instead of placing the pot on top of the stove, put it in a 350° oven for about 25 minutes, or until all the liquid has been absorbed.

To make a better seal: cut waxed paper to size slightly larger than size of pot, punch a small hole in the center, cover pot with paper. Set the lid on this and cook as above, either on top of the stove or in the oven.

For a nutty-flavored rice: brown uncooked rice in hot butter, lightly, in a heavy skillet, stirring constantly until light tan in color. Then cook according to the absorption method, above.

For a dry rice: after rice is cooked, toss it lightly and place it in a warm oven for about 5 minutes.

to serve: serve rice in a heated bowl or on a heated platter to avoid gumminess.

leftover rice: rinse with hot water and drain and dry well to separate the grains, then add to pancake, waffle or muffin batter; make rice puddings; croquettes; mix with meat for stuffed green peppers or stuffed cabbage, or meat loaf.

pre-cooked (converted) rice: this type of rice cannot be cooked down to a cream for use in desserts.

wild rice: (*this is really a grass, not a rice*): Wild rice triples in bulk when cooked. It should be rinsed many times before cooking, and then soaked for 15 minutes before being placed on a flame. It requires longer cooking than white or brown rice.

ROASTS:

TIPS

- when ordering a boned roast, ask your butcher for the bones, for soups and gravies.
- a small roast requires more minutes per pound in cooking than does a large one.
- a coating of fat should always be left on (or if necessary, added to) meat when it is roasting. It bastes the meat and prevents drying out.
- always baste a roast frequently (buy a long-handled basting spoon for this) and turn often, if possible. Add liquid only as necessary, and a little at a time, to prevent steaming the meat.
- a large roast of any kind should be removed from the oven when done and kept warm for about 15 minutes before being carved. Less juice will be lost.
- if you use aluminum foil in the oven, don't cover the entire rack or bottom completely, otherwise you will interfere with the proper distribution of heat.

ROLLS (see also BREAD):

for a beautiful amber crust: dissolve one bouillon cube in ½ cup boiling water and brush the rolls with this before putting them in the oven.

to save time when preparing rolls for a dinner for guests, bake rolls several days ahead of time and place them in the freezer. Heat in the oven just before serving.

to freshen stale rolls and biscuits: dip them quickly in cold water and heat to crispness in a hot oven. This can be done only once.

ROMAINE (see LETTUCE)

ROTISSERIE BROILING (see BROILING)

RUBBER HOUSEHOLD GLOVES: these are indispensable for the handling of hot vegetables like baked potatoes, or of hard-to-handle foods such as artichokes or pineapples, quite apart from their usual uses in dishwashing, etc.

S

SACCHARIN: some low-calorie sweeteners have a slightly unpleasant after taste. Preferable to pure saccharin are those products which are a blend of lactose, calcium cyclamate and saccharin: read the labels.

SALAD (see also LETTUCE):

TIPS

- greens for salads can be washed, then kept crisp for several hours in the refrigerator if wrapped in a soft absorbent towel. This also serves to remove excess water.
- better still, toss well-drained greens with a small amount of oil so that every leaf is lightly coated, then refrigerate in a large plastic bag. The greens will stay much crisper.
- tear salad greens into pieces instead of cutting with a knife, to keep the edges from turning dark.

salad ingredients: use the following in salads:

- fresh green celery leaves
- raw, firm white sliced mushroom caps
- raw baby spinach leaves (the tender inside portion of a clump of fresh spinach)
- nasturtium leaves and flowers, if you have them in your garden or window box; they are a member of the cress family, and deliciously pungent. (Don't use any which have been sprayed with insecticides.)
- sweet white onion slices which have been blanched and chilled

salad dressings: if you like to add oil and vinegar separately to salad greens, always add the oil first. Oil will not cling to a salad leaf which has been wet with vinegar.

TIPS

- a translation from the French: be a miser with the vinegar, a philanthropist with the oil, a madman with the mixing.
- as indicated above, avoid using too much vinegar or lemon juice in proportion to the amount of oil. A good rule of thumb is to use 1 tablespoon of flavored or wine vinegar (or lemon juice) to 3 or more of oil. One to 4 is often preferred.
- a pinch of sugar added to most homemade dressings is all to the good.
- try substituting lime juice occasionally for vinegar in dressings.
- the liquid from mustard pickles is often excellent as a substitute for vinegar in dressings. So is the liquid from sweet pickles, in moderate amounts.
- most salad dressings should be served at room temperature (but the salads, of course, should be chilled).

SALAD BOWLS:

to season: use unfinished wooden bowls, rub inside and outside with salad oil until the surfaces can absorb no more. Let stand overnight. Wipe dry and use. Bowls thus prepared can be washed like any other bowl (but do not soak). Give them an occasional oil rubbing, a few times a year.

SALT:

in cooking: salt helps to extract the juices from meat, so when making meat soups, or chicken soups, add it to the liquid early. Conversely, don't use salt during the initial cooking of roasts, chops or steaks, so that their juices will not be coaxed out. Add the salt shortly before serving time.

TIP

- salt toughens eggs, so add it to egg dishes only after they are cooked.

to remove excess salt: add slices of raw potato to a cooking liquid which is too salty, and cook until the potato is parboiled (begins to become translucent). The quantity of potato depends upon the degree of excess saltiness. Remove the potato with a slotted spoon or small strainer. Don't let the potato cook too long or it will break and become difficult to remove.

TIP

- a slight excess of salt can often be disguised by adding a small amount of sugar. If sugar is taboo in the dish, try a bit of vinegar.

to clean omelet pans: coarse salt tied in a square of gauze will remove egg remnants from a cast-iron pan. Use oil with it, never water.

in pickling: use plain—not iodized—salt.

to bed hot oysters and clams in the half shell: heated coarse salt is often used for the placing of preparations like clams casino, oysters Delmonico, etc. The salt holds heat well and keeps them piping hot during the serving and eating, and also stabilizes them in the dish.

to prevent a cracked egg from breaking: if an egg cracks while boiling, immediately pour a large quantity of salt on the crack (lowering the flame first). This often serves to seal the egg.

SANDWICHES:

bread: if you like extra-thin bread slices for sandwiches, freeze a loaf of unsliced bread and you will be able to cut slices as thin as you wish.

TIP

- very fresh bread is hard to spread for sandwiches. Day-old bread is best, or store-bought bread which has been exposed to air for a few hours.

For rolled sandwiches: very fresh bread is excellent for rolled sandwiches or canapés. Cut off the crusts before rolling; also, wrap them in a moist cloth before chilling.

spreads: cream the butter to be used for sandwiches. It spreads more evenly and goes further.

TIPS

- 1 stick of softened butter will spread about 25 slices of bread.
- 1 pint of mayonnaise will spread about 50 slices of bread.
- 1 cup of sandwich filling will usually make about 6 sandwiches.

to make sandwiches in advance: leave the crusts on when making sandwiches to be stored; this helps prevent their drying out.

TIPS

- sandwiches with moist fillings should *not* be prepared far in advance—the bread becomes soggy.
- prepared sandwiches can be kept for 24 hours in the refrigerator if very well wrapped, either in 2 thicknesses of dish towels, or in a plastic bag.
- sandwiches (without mayonnaise or lettuce) can be made and frozen for future use. If removed from the freezer in the morning, they will be ready to eat at lunchtime.

SAUCES:

to cook: any sauce containing mustard or eggs must not be boiled, for it will curdle. Cook in a double boiler over hot (not boiling) water.

If it curdles: if a sauce containing eggs begins to curdle due to excess heat, pour it at once into a cold dish and beat hard with a whisk.

Hollandaise: if the mixture curdles, beat in with a whisk 2 tablespoons of heavy sweet cream or 1 whipped egg yolk.

Cream sauce: this is easily scorched if cooked over direct heat. Make this in a double boiler over hot (not boiling) water.

Thickeners: a better thickener than flour in a sauce is egg yolks: one, or better still, two. They make a sauce velvety, without a floury taste. (See EGGS, *yolks*)

TIP

- for a clear sauce thickener, use cornstarch, arrowroot or potato starch.

for fish: a court bouillon (seasoned water in which fish has been poached) makes an excellent base for any sauce to be served on fish. Simmer the liquid until it is reduced to the desired amount or strength.

to make up ahead of time: any thickened mixture containing starch or egg yolks will, upon cooling, develop a skin. To prevent this, stir the mixture from time to time with a wire whisk as it cools. Then cover with plastic wrap or wax paper, immediately upon the surface.

sauces from leftovers: if you have a little leftover soup, run it through the blender or vegetable mill, or push it through a sieve: use this purée as a sauce base for meats, chicken or vegetables.

- most leftover fish, meats or vegetables can be puréed and used as a sauce base.

to serve leftovers with: many leftovers, served with an unusual sauce, can become delicious appetizers, or side dishes with a meal.

for a low-calorie sauce (see ONIONS, *for a low calorie sauce*)

SAUERKRAUT: this is a neglected dish. Serve it hot, for a change: toss with a little bacon fat or chopped crisp bacon. Try adding some caraway seeds to it, hot or cold. Or (for serving cold) some ice-cold cranberries, cut in half.

SAUSAGE:

GENERAL TIPS

- some sausages contain cereal as well as pork meat. Know which ones you are buying.
- since sausages consist largely or wholly of pork, they must be well cooked, never pink inside.

to keep from bursting or shriveling: cook them slowly and turn them frequently.

or

Parboil them for a few minutes; then drain and roll in flour. Then fry.

to make less greasy: put sausages in a cold frying pan with, of course, no added fat. This also makes them more tender.

SAUTÉEING: if you use oil for sautéeing, add a small amount of solid fat also, to make browning easier and faster.

SCALES: weights are more dependable than measures. They are also easier to work with, as when measuring solid fats. If you wish to eliminate even the possibility of a variable result in certain dishes, invest in a kitchen scale. Convert your measures (in your favorite recipes, especially) to ounces or grams.

SCALLIONS: the white part of scallions (also known as green onions) are a good substitute for shallots if you cannot buy the latter.

SCALLOPS:

to buy: scallops are almost always sold out of their shells, by the pound. Bay scallops are small, cream-colored and tender: they have a more delicate flavor (and are more expensive) than sea scallops—larger, often whiter, slightly tougher, but still excellent.

to prepare: after washing, sprinkle scallops with lemon juice and let stand for 20 minutes.

to cook: regardless of cooking method, remember not to cook scallops overlong. Like all shellfish they toughen quickly in the presence of heat.

SCISSORS: keep a sharp scissors in the kitchen for use in cutting foods only. They are handier than a knife for cutting fresh dill, chives, raw bacon.

SCORCHED FOOD: if food is not badly scorched, you can eliminate most of the burned flavor by immediately setting the scorched pan in a little cold water before turning the contents (without scraping) into another pan.

SERVING PLATES: heat dishes and platters in which hot foods are to be served, in a low oven first. This keeps fried foods from becoming soggy, and keeps the food from losing its heat during the table serving.

SHALLOTS: this small bulbous herb seems midway between an onion and a head of garlic: it is excellent for stews, soups and salads. Shallots will keep for months in the bottom vegetable bin of the refrigerator if they are kept dry and exposed to air.

SHELLFISH (see CLAMS, CRABS, LOBSTERS, MUSSELS, etc.)

SHERRY (see WINES)

SHOPPING LIST: buy a roll of adding machine paper and hang it on your kitchen wall with a string and pencil attached close by. Write needed items as they occur, then tear off the necessary portion each time you go on a shopping trip.

SHRIMP:

to buy: the shells of raw shrimp should fit the body closely; shrinkage is usually a sign of staleness. Raw shrimp are grayish-green in color, cooked shrimp are pink. In general, the small shrimp are better flavored and more delicate than the larger ones.

to peel: shrimp are more easily peeled and deveined when raw than when cooked. If you have no shrimp peeler, shell a shrimp by removing the legs and tail first, then lift off the entire covering.

to clean: remove the intestinal vein (along the back of the shrimp) by using the blunt end of a toothpick, under cold running water.

to cook: wash the shells after they have been removed, then place them in the cooking water (bound in cheesecloth, if you wish) for added flavor.

TIPS

- the flavor of shrimp is well brought out if they are cooked in salted water with peppercorns, thyme, bay leaf and parsley. A little white wine never hurts.
- shrimp which is simmered (unpeeled) in beer has an interesting flavor, a little similar to lobster.

canned: soak canned shrimp for 5 minutes in cold water before using in place of fresh-cooked shrimp. This helps to eliminate the canned flavor.

SIFTING (see also FLOUR):

flour: a short-cut which flies in the face of stern tradition: when a recipe calls for a certain number of cups of sifted flour—and you are either lazy or rushed—measure the flour straight from the canister, remove about 1 tablespoon from each cupful, and sift the remainder into the final bowl, as though you had already sifted it before measuring. The resulting amount of sifted flour seems right for most uses, and the dough or batter comes out fine. One note, though: don't use this method when a recipe insists that the flour be sifted two or three times.

brown sugar: sift brown sugar by pushing it through a rather coarse strainer with the bowl of a spoon. Don't use a flour sifter for this.

SINK STAINS: tea, coffee, beet, onionskin, etc., stains can be removed from porcelain-finished sinks by washing with laundry bleach, followed by a water rinse.

SLICING (see KNIVES): use a sharp French chef's knife for slicing vegetables. Some cooks prefer a sharp saw-toothed knife, using a quick, sawing motion.

for uniform thickness: to slice onions, bread, cabbage, tomatoes, etc.: rotate the food slightly after each slice is cut. This decreases the common tendency to end up slicing on the diagonal.

SOLE (see also FISH):

to buy: the fish called "sole" in the United States is not the same as the true English, or Dover, sole. It is, however, a delicious fish in its own right. "Lemon sole" comes from Florida, "gray sole" from Canada. These two are softer-fleshed fish than English sole. Flounder is sometimes called sole, and is much like sole in taste and texture.

- the underside of the flounder has white meat, the upper is slightly gray in color. This is why a tray of flounder (sometimes misnamed sole) fillets at the fish market contains fillets of two different colors. There is no detectable difference in taste.

SOUFFLÉ:

batter: beaten egg whites should be folded gently into soufflé batter, not mixed, so that as much air is retained as possible.

TIP

- diluted evaporated milk is excellent as a substitute for fresh milk in soufflés; it actually improves the flavor.

to bake:

To avoid spilling: a soufflé will not spill over in the oven if, after you pour the batter into the mold, you run your finger around the top, between the mold and the batter, about ½ an inch deep.

For a soft soufflé: place the filled mold in an outer pan of hot water, then set in oven.

For a crusty soufflé: place the mold in the oven without an outer pan of hot water.

to keep from falling: never open the oven door, not even a crack, while a soufflé is baking. And since it falls within a few minutes of removal from the oven, time it so that you can serve it at once.

cheese soufflé: a dry, not too fatty cheese is best for a soufflé. Store cheese (natural cheddar), a dry Swiss or Parmesan cheese are the most commonly used.

To dry out an oily cheese: set the piece of cheese on a piece of paper toweling and let it stand several days. Change the toweling from time to time as it absorbs the oil.

soufflé for dessert: butter the mold and sprinkle it with sugar before pouring in the batter. The soufflé will come neatly from the mold and will have a fine sweet crust.

SOUP (see also STOCK):

TIPS

- excellent bones for soup are leg bones and knuckles. Have your butcher cut them up or saw them into medium-size pieces. You will get more out of them.
- never throw steak bones, bones from roasts, or chicken carcasses away until you have extracted all the good from them, in the form of a soup or stock. If you don't feel like making soup out of some bones on hand, wrap them well and put them in the freezer until you do feel like making soup.
- save all vegetable juices from cooked or canned vegetables, mushrooms, etc., to use in soups. You can freeze these, too, until you are ready to use them.

to cook: cover ingredients with cold water and cook (never boil rapidly) for hours, if possible, at low heat, skimming off any material which rises to the top. A small tea strainer is good for this. Because soup should simmer long, start soup-making early in the day, or the day before.

TIPS

- to extract the most from meat and bones in soup, add salt to the water at the beginning of cooking.
- vegetables added to meat soups should be put in the pot toward the end of cooking so that they will not become over-soft; they will also produce a tastier soup if they are gently sautéed first, preferably in butter.

For a rich golden color: brown chicken or meat in the oven or on top of the stove, before adding to soup. (Naturally this improves flavor too.) Bones should also be browned in the oven first, for the best flavor.

- mix 1 tablespoon sugar with 1 tablespoon water and heat until the water evaporates and the sugar begins to brown. Add to the soup. Double or triple this, depending on the amount of soup.

fish soups: soups and chowders are 100 per cent improved if you use the shells and bones when preparing fish stock. Cook shrimp and cracked lobster shells, fish heads and bones in water, then strain carefully.

thickening: put cooked vegetables in a blender or through a sieve, then add to soup.

- mix ½ cup cornstarch with ¼ cup sherry and add some or all of this to the soup, depending on the desired amount of thickness.

cream soups: use chicken stock or chicken consommé for a delicate base to cream soups.

TIP

- use undiluted evaporated milk as part of the liquid in cream soups for a richer consistency.

cold soups: any soup to be served cold must have all traces of fat removed. Congealed fat in a chilled soup is unpleasant in taste and texture.

- a cold soup should always be thoroughly chilled—prepare and refrigerate the day before, if possible.

jellied soups: soups will jell naturally (upon chilling) if they have been made with bones. The best bones to use for this are cracked veal knuckles and chicken feet. For clear jellied soups, strain and refrigerate.

- to get an ordinary liquid soup to jell, add 1 tablespoon of gelatin for each 2 cups of liquid. (Soften gelatin in a small amount of cold liquid first.)

leftover soups: throw almost any kind of soup into a blender to get a sauce or gravy for vegetables or meat.

to remove fat: fat can be removed from hot soup by floating one or more lettuce leaves on the surface, removing and adding more when they have absorbed the grease.

wine in soup: a little Burgundy is delicious in borscht, a bit of sherry in consommé—almost any good dry white or red wine, in small quantity, will help a soup.

SOUR CREAM (see CREAM)

SPAGHETTI, NOODLES, ETC.: these about double in volume when cooked. Eight ounces will serve 3 or 4 people.

to boil: add 1 tablespoon of vegetable or olive oil to the boiling water. This helps prevent spaghetti, etc., from sticking together, or sticking to the pot, and also helps keep the contents from boiling over.

- immerse gradually in rapidly boiling water so as not to disturb the boiling point. They will then cook evenly.

to prepare ahead of time: cook, drain, then place spaghetti, etc., in the refrigerator. Before serving, immerse for a minute or two in water which has been brought to a boil. (It is best to leave the spaghetti a very little on the firm side in your first cooking.)

SPICES: keep a small jar containing a mixture of salt, pepper, paprika, powdered garlic or onion, and any herbs you like, in the refrigerator. This is handy and quick for seasoning meat, chicken and fish. It keeps indefinitely, if refrigerated.

SPINACH:

to cook: add no water when you cook spinach—the water which adheres to the washed leaves is enough. Spinach cooks quickly—cover, but do not overcook it. Lift the cover a few times during cooking and it will stay a bright green.

in salad: tender baby leaves of raw spinach make a delicate salad green to be served alone or mixed with other greens.

creamed, boiled: add some grated nutmeg. Mix into it some hard-boiled egg yolks pushed through a sieve.

SPONGE CAKE: add a few drops of anise to sponge cake batter.

SPOONS: the most useful spoons in the kitchen are a set of long-handled wooden ones. Use for all kinds of stirring where a whisk will not do—in pots on the stove, thick cake batters, etc.

measuring spoons: keep a plastic set of measuring spoons on a ring in each of your canisters—flour, sugar, salt, etc. Use, then replace in canister, without frequent need of washing.

SQUASH:

varieties: there are 2 main types of squash:

(1) the hard-fleshed winter squash: butternut, acorn and hubbard, in which generally only the flesh is eaten. They are pumpkin-like in texture and color of the flesh, and are generally served baked, boiled, mashed or in pies.

(2) the soft-skinned, soft-fleshed varieties: yellow summer squash, crook-necked, and the green zucchini. The entire squash can be eaten, seeds and skins included, and may be mashed, sautéed, or halved and baked.

suggestions: squash has an affinity for ginger. Peeled, boiled, mashed butternut squash is delicious if served with a heaping tablespoonful of ginger marmalade well mixed into it. Not even butter is needed.

or

Scrub acorn squash, cut it in half and seed it, then bake in the oven with a teaspoon of ginger marmalade placed in the center of each half.

STEAK (see BEEF)

STEWS:

TIPS

- all stews (and thick soups) taste better the day after they are made.
- don't put too much liquid in the stew pot—only enough barely to cover the contents. To avoid having it boil away too soon, cut a sheet of wax paper the size of the pot, make a tiny hole in the center, and cover the stew with this. Then put on the lid. Cook over a slow flame.

vegetables: vegetables in a stew taste much better if they are lightly sautéed in butter first.

- since vegetables have different cooking times, combine them with the meats in the proper order so that the softer ones have not cooked to mushiness by the time the tougher ones (or the meats) are done.

meats: when you brown pieces of meat for stew, put only a few pieces at a time in the browning pan; too many at once produces steam which spoils the color and flavor of the meat.

TIP

- meats brown better in pans with low sides, such as skillets.

to freeze: don't add vegetables to a stew which you intend to freeze. They usually become mushy upon thawing. Make the stew, omitting the vegetables or serving them as a vegetable course that day. Add fresh vegetables to the stew when it has been defrosted, and cook together only until the vegetables are done.

STOCK (see also SOUP):

TIP

- whenever a meat or chicken recipe calls for adding water, add some of your stock instead.

to make: you can almost always have some sort of stock on hand in the refrigerator or freezer by following these pointers: never throw away meat or chicken bones until you have simmered them for a couple of hours. Strain the liquid and cook down to desired strength. Add all liquids from cooked and canned vegetables (except members of the cabbage family) to your stock pot and simmer again. Add leftover gravies to the stock pot. Add chicken feet. Add giblets.

TIPS

- when stock has reached the desired strength, remove the large bones and vegetables with a slotted spoon, throw in ½ cup of cold water, and let stand for 10 minutes. The sediment will go to the bottom and removal of the clear liquid is easier.
- keep a jar of juices drained from vegetables, leftover gravies, etc., in your freezer, and keep adding to it until the jar is almost filled (leave room for expansion upon freezing). If you replace the jar in the freezer at once (label it!) it will keep indefinitely. Once the jar is filled, you have a marvelous soup stock, practically ready to serve upon thawing.
- save the water in which you soak dried mushrooms; it makes an excellent stock for gravy bases and some sauces.

to clarify: stir into the stock 1 egg white beaten with 2 teaspoons of water plus the eggshell broken into small bits: this for each quart of stock. Boil up for about 2 minutes, then strain through several thicknesses of cheesecloth draped over a large strainer.

to store: stock can be stored for a week in the refrigerator if it contains enough fat to rise, congeal and coat the surface. Cold fat is easily removed from refrigerated stock.

TIPS

- stock can be stored indefinitely if you remove it from the refrigerator every 3 days and boil it up briskly for 10 minutes, adding a little water or other liquid to replace that lost from evaporation during boiling. Replace in refrigerator.
- stock can be boiled down and concentrated so that it occupies little storage space in the refrigerator. When

ready to use, add sufficient water to bring it up to required strength.

fish stock (see also SOUPS, *fish soup*): fish stock doesn't have to be made from fish only. Slip in a beef or veal bone in the early part of cooking; it gives a richer flavor.

STORAGE:

containers: save jars of all sizes which have tight screw-tops, for storing leftovers, etc. Attach a strip of white plastic tape to each cover and pencil on it what the jar contains. The writing erases easily, and the tapes survive many washings. (Glass jars can go into the freezer, provided you remember to leave room inside for expansion during freezing. To defrost foods stored in glass jars, set the jars in *cold* water until the contents have loosened.)

TIP

- excellent containers for storing noodles, spaghetti, etc., are the large-size glass jars which instant coffee comes in.

foods: most foods deteriorate or lose flavor and potency if kept overlong on the pantry shelf. These include almost all starches: bread and cracker crumbs, beans, split peas, flour, spaghetti products, baking powder, herbs. Unless you bake a great deal, buy the smaller sizes of baking powder and flour.

STRINGBEANS (see BEANS)

STUFFING (see BIRDS)

SUGAR:

granulated: one pound of granulated sugar equals 2 cups.

For searing: use a little sugar to sear meat to a beautiful brown: add 1 tablespoon sugar to heated fat, stir until the sugar browns (over a moderate-to-high flame), add the meat and cook, turning meat on all sides until uniformly dark. This adds no detectable sweetness to the meat.

In place of salt: for low-salt diets, add a little sugar to the cooking water for vegetables, to make them more palatable.

In meringues: never add sugar to beaten egg whites until they stand up in peaks; then add it gradually, beating well between additions.

To make vanilla-flavored sugar: place 8 or 10 whole vanilla pods in a quart wide-mouthed jar with a tight screw cap. Fill the jar three fourths full with sugar, screw cap on tightly, shake, then store on your pantry shelf. Use this sugar for cake batter (omitting vanilla extract) and your cakes will have an old-fashioned vanilla flavor. Don't mind the little black specks in the sugar—they are supposed to be there. Replace the sugar in the jar whenever necessary, shaking well before storing again. The vanilla pods will last for years.

For dessert soufflés: sprinkle sugar over the surface of the buttered mold before pouring in the soufflé batter. This gives a fine sweet crust.

confectioners' sugar: one pound of confectioners' (powdered) sugar equals 3½ cups, sifted.

To dust with sugar: to dust cakes, cookies, puddings, etc., place confectioners' sugar in a strainer and turn the sugar about with a spoon, pressing gently.

- when dusting moist cakes, wait until just before serving to do so. Confectioners' sugar turns grayish when it stands on a moist surface.
- *for doughnuts:* put sugar in a paper bag and shake the doughnuts in this, one at a time.

brown sugar: one pound brown sugar equals 2¼ cups, firmly packed.

To measure: the old-fashioned types of brown sugar (light or dark) must always be packed down firmly in cups and spoons, when measuring. There is a new granulated brown sugar available now which is measured and handled much like white sugar. You must decide whether the convenience afforded by the new type is worth the extra price.

To sift: use a coarse-meshed strainer and push the sugar through briskly with the side and bottom of a spoon. Don't sift brown sugar in a flour sifter—it will gum up the works.

To store: keep brown sugar in a jar with a tight screw cap. Don't leave brown sugar exposed to air, or it will harden.

To soften: if brown sugar cakes and becomes hard, enclose half an apple or else a slice of bread in it, close tightly, and allow to stand overnight. Remove the apple or slice of bread the next day. The moisture from the apple or bread will have uncaked the sugar.

To use in cakes or cookies: if you use brown sugar to replace all or part of white sugar in a cake recipe, use some baking soda to counteract the acidity, or the cake will not rise properly. (¾ teaspoon of soda to 1 cup of brown sugar is about right.)

SWEETBREADS: always blanch these before cooking. A second cooking (simmered in seasoned broth for 20 minutes) before their final preparation tenderizes and flavors them further.

SWEET POTATOES: sweet potatoes and yams should not be stored overlong as they do not keep well. Use them within two days after buying.

SWISS CHARD: like spinach, chard needs no extra water in cooking, beyond that which clings to the leaves after washing. But it needs slightly longer cooking. Avoid salt in the cooking water—it tends to turn swiss chard dark.

SYRUPS:

in measuring: before pouring syrup into a measuring cup or spoon, oil the inside of the receptacle. Syrup pours from the cup more easily, leaving little behind.

• always clean off the neck of the syrup bottle with a clean damp cloth before replacing cover. This makes it easy to open the next time.

in icings: for use in a cake icing, take care not to overcook the syrup. It must be cooked only to the soft-ball stage, or the icing will have a fudgy consistency and be difficult to spread.

maple syrup:

To buy: most brands of "maple" syrup are a mixture of maple and cane syrups. Read the labels, know which you are getting. (For pancakes, there is nothing quite like 100 per cent maple syrup.)

- the finer grades of pure maple syrup are very light in color. Cheaper grades (still good) are darker and less delicate in flavor.

To store: keep maple syrup in a cool dark place. Once the bottle is opened, store it in the refrigerator to prevent fermentation. Should fermentation occur (bubbles, and grayish scum on top), strain syrup into a pan, heat to boiling, and allow to boil for one minute. Skim it and strain again into a hot clean jar. This will practically restore it to its former condition.

T

TAPIOCA PUDDING: if the pudding is sticky, you have cooked it too long.

TEA:

to make: use freshly boiled water when making tea. Tea should be steeped about 5 minutes before serving. Use a pottery or china teapot, but first heat it by pouring boiling water into it, rinse out, then add the tea leaves and cover with boiling water.

iced: iced tea may become cloudy, but this does not affect its flavor.

For non-cloudy iced tea pour 1 quart cold water over 4 teaspoons of tea leaves in a glass or china container and allow to stand about 12 hours in the refrigerator. Strain before serving. This is clear and strong.

or

Make strong tea, cool it at room temperature, then pour when cooled over ice cubes.

TEFLON-LINED PANS (see POTS and PANS)

THICKENING:

flour: when using flour to thicken gravies, soups, etc., mix it with a small amount of hot melted fat first. The flour will mix more easily into the hot liquid, and the flavor is improved: it will not have a "floury" taste.

TIP

- if flour alone must be added to a hot liquid, mix it first with a few tablespoons of the liquid in a cup, using a whisk or a fork and mixing until smooth. Then add this thin paste slowly to the pot, mixing well as you add.

cornstarch: cornstarch gives a clear quality to a soup or sauce, whereas flour makes it opaque. One tablespoon of cornstarch equals 2 tablespoons of flour in thickening power.

arrowroot: like cornstarch, arrowroot will thicken without making the mixture cloudy. Use slightly less than you would if cornstarch were used.

egg yolks: one or two beaten egg yolks are preferred as a thickener for most sauces. They produce a more delicate sauce, with no starchy taste. But take care not to let the mixture approach boiling, or it will curdle. Add the hot liquid, 1 tablespoon at a time, to the yolks, until you have a velvety cream. Then add this to the remainder of the hot liquid, mixing well as you add.

puréed onions or vegetables: these are excellent as a soup or sauce thickener, and are less starchy than arrowroot, cornstarch or flour.

TOMATOES:

to ripen: place green or unripened tomatoes in a brown paper bag and place in a dark spot for 3 or 4 days, depending on the degree of greenness. Don't put tomatoes in the sun to ripen—this softens them.

to peel: bring a pot of water to the boiling point, turn it off and place tomatoes in it. Remove them in a minute or two, when the skins begin to shrivel. You can pull the skins off easily with a firm downward pull.

or

Hold tomato over a gas flame on a fork, turning until the skin begins to shrivel.

or

If the tomato is firm, rub the skin gently with a knife handle, then split carefully and peel.

to remove seeds: cut tomato in half crosswise and hold the cut side under running water, using your fingers to help push out the seeds.

in salad: tomatoes which have been cut lengthwise will lose less juice than if cut crosswise.

TIP

- add tomatoes last to the salad, as a garnish, otherwise their juices will dilute the dressing and make the salad soggy.

TOMATO PASTE, PURÉE AND SAUCE:

tomato paste is concentrated puréed tomato seasoned with salt. It can also be purchased without salt. Keep several small cans on your pantry shelf and dilute to taste for tomato purée, tomato sauce and—for cooking—tomato juice. Add flavorings. This is a saving of shelf space and money.

tomato purée is unseasoned tomato sauce.

tomato sauce is puréed tomato seasoned with salt, pepper and spices.

TONGUE (see also BEEF):

to peel: tongue should be peeled while it is hot. One tablespoon of vinegar added to the last water in which it is cooked will make peeling easier.

TOOLS: when buying kitchen tools, avoid those with painted wooden handles. The paint tends to peel, in time, often flaking off into the food being prepared.

TROUT (see also FISH):

to eliminate fishy flavor: skin a trout before cooking by cutting the skin all the way around behind the head. Grasp skin with a dry cloth to eliminate slipping, and pull straight back. You can also rub salt on your fingers to prevent slipping.

TRUSSING (see BIRDS)

TUNA FISH (see also BONITO):

canned: tuna is available in flake, chunk and solid-pack forms. The solid pack is a continuous piece or slice of the fish, more expensive than the other two. But flake or chunk are fine for salads or any dish calling for tuna well mixed with other ingredients.

Solid pack: solid pack tuna comes in 3 grades: white, light, and dark meat. The white is favored for its flavor, and is the most expensive. The light and dark meats, however, are also excellent in almost any tuna dish.

White meat tuna fish in solid-pack form is an excellent substitute for chicken in salads and curry dishes. If properly prepared, it is sometimes difficult to tell it from chicken. To use tuna for this purpose, drain it, soak in cold water for 10 minutes, then drain again well. (You must use white meat tuna for this deception.)

TURKEY (see also BIRDS):

to buy: an ideal-sized turkey for most families is about 10 pounds. A fresh turkey is preferable to a frozen one, if you remember to order it from your butcher ahead of time. Frozen turkeys are generally satisfactory, however, but you must allow approximately one day for thorough defrosting. Directions for this are usually on the package.

To determine age of a fresh turkey: a young turkey has black feet; a medium-aged turkey has pink feet; an old turkey has gray feet.

to roast: turkeys and other large birds requiring long cooking should be well oiled or larded with fat, particularly on the breast, for they tend to become dry. Baste often.

To stuff: stuff a turkey lightly. You may use the heel of a loaf of bread to hold the stuffing in, if the cavity opening is large. (See BIRDS, *stuffing*)

TIPS

- you can use dental floss instead of thread to sew up a stuffed turkey—it holds better.

- lay a stuffed turkey on its side in the oven until the top side begins to brown. Then turn it to the other side. A half hour before removing it from the oven, place it on its back to allow the breast to brown. A turkey roasted in this manner is cooked evenly, down to the last bit of stuffing.

Test for doneness: grasp the drumstick by the end and move it gently. If it moves easily, or breaks from the carcass, the bird is done.

broiled: a very young turkey may be broiled, like chicken. Broil under a medium flame. Add a few tablespoons of water to the broiler pan after turning the turkey, to prevent scorching.

bones: save all turkey bones after the bird is eaten. Throw them into your soup or stock pot, or brew up a rich stock for future use.

TURNIPS: these are a much neglected vegetable. Boil them and serve them mashed, with butter and nutmeg—or cubed, with cubed cooked carrots. A little sherry added just before serving gives a fine touch.

TIP

- turnips are sweeter if they are not skinned before they are cooked.

V

VANILLA (see SUGAR, *to make vanilla-flavored sugar*)

VEAL (see also LIVER, MEATS, ROASTS, STEWS, TONGUE):

general: calves' meat is light in color because the animals are milk-fed. As they get older and start eating grass the flesh becomes reddish and has a different taste.

- since veal is delicately flavored, don't use strongly flavored vegetables with it.

roast: veal contains less fat than beef, therefore it dries more easily in cooking. Cover a veal roast with thin strips of fat (this is called larding a roast) and cook more slowly than beef.

chops: to give chops a nice butter flavor without danger of burning the butter, sauté them with oil or other fat as you normally would, but add a small amount of butter to the pan a few minutes before the chops are done. Turn them once after the butter has been added.

To broil: spread floured veal chops with a little melted butter before broiling to give them a golden color.

for gravies, etc.: a veal bone (shank, knuckle, etc.) gives a marvelous flavor to a gravy base or soup stock. Ask the butcher to split the bone.

VEGETABLES (see also separate headings, as BRUSSELS SPROUTS, CABBAGE, etc., see also PEELING VEGETABLES):

to buy: with some few exceptions, the smaller and younger vegetables are preferable to the large mature ones. Tender vegetables, no matter how prepared, have twice the flavor of tough ones.

leafy vegetables: vegetables which may harbor insects should be soaked in well-salted cold water for about half an hour. Do this with broccoli, Brussels sprouts, artichokes, curled leaf lettuce, etc.

To store: wrap washed vegetables in paper toweling and place in the vegetable compartment of the refrigerator. The moisture adhering is just enough to keep them fresh for several days.

root vegetables: cut the greens from vegetables with leafy tops (beets, carrots, turnips, parsnips) before storing them; otherwise their juices continue to be drawn from the root into the leaves.

to serve raw: carrots, celery, onions, etc., should be soaked in ice water for about 20 minutes before being served.

to keep their color: potatoes or eggplant or other vegetables which tend to darken after being peeled should be placed in water as you peel them.

to cook: Americans tend to overcook most vegetables (so do the British). Hats off to the Chinese and the French, who know that vegetables, when cooked, should be fairly firm, even slightly crunchy, to the teeth; never mushy.

In liquid: most vegetables taste better and are more nutritious if cooked in very little liquid, often just enough so that there is barely any left in the pot after cooking. It is better to add a bit of liquid from time to time than to have the vegetables swimming in it.

To retain vitamins: vegetables keep their vitamin content better in slightly acid solutions, so add a bit of lemon juice to the cooking water.

TIP

- use salt last in cooking vegetables, for it tends to leach out vitamins.

To tenderize: simmer tough vegetables in milk instead of water. Don't mind if the milk curdles slightly.

To sauté: keep your eye on the pan—sautéed vegetables can be the most delicious of all methods of preparation, but they are terrible if cooked to mushiness.

TIP

- if the vegetables are tough mature ones, parboil them before sautéeing.

Chinese method: sauté vegetables quickly in a small amount of hot oil, then finish cooking with a small amount of added liquid, remembering to leave them slightly crisp.

Creamed: use evaporated milk instead of fresh milk for richer flavor in your cream sauces.

Canned: heat canned vegetables to the simmering point only, before serving.

dehydrated vegetables: keep packages of dehydrated vegetable flakes in the pantry for quickly available additions to soups and stews. Soak them for about 10 minutes in a very small amount of water first to bring out the flavor and to cook them more quickly and uniformly.

W

WAFFLES:

waffle iron: if using a new waffle iron for the first time, put a little extra shortening in the batter to temper the iron.

To test for readiness to use: heat the iron, put in 1 teaspoonful of water, then close it. When the steaming stops, the iron is at the right temperature to use.

batter: use no sugar in waffle batter, otherwise the waffle will not be crisp. (If you *like* soft waffles, add a bit of sugar when mixing the batter.)

to freeze: if you have mixed more batter than you need, make the waffles and put them in the freezer. Toast them when you want them, without thawing.

WALNUTS:

in the shell: walnuts in the shell will last well for about 6 months.

shelled: shelled walnuts will keep well at room temperature for about 1 month; they will keep fresh in the refrigerator for about 3 months; they will keep indefinitely (if airtight) in the freezer.

to use as a garnish or in salads, etc.: soak shelled walnuts several hours in salted water, then pat dry.

WARMING PLATES: to prevent the possible cracking of serving plates when placed in the oven to warm, spread brown paper over the surface on which they are to be set.

WATERCRESS:

to store: wash watercress, then stand it upright, the stems in a glass of cold water. Wrap the whole in a plastic bag and refrigerate. Fresh cress will keep for about a week this way.

to use: outside of its use in salads and for garnishing, watercress is delicious in soup. Mince it, and cook it in cream soups. It can also be served in clear bouillons.

WAXED PAPER: waxed paper used for rolling out pie dough, cookies, etc., will not slip if you place it on a wet surface.

WHIPPED CREAM (see CREAM, *whipped*)

WINE:

TIP

- if you have discovered a bottle of wine which you like very much, and if you don't find it too expensive, buy a case of it from your dealer. It is almost always cheaper by the case. You can generally count on its remaining good for at least a year. If in doubt, ask your dealer.

what goes with what: as is well known, dry white wines with their light flavors are usually served with fish, seafood, poultry and light meats; red wines, more robust, with red meat and game; pink wines, (rosé) generally with all types of food. But if you want to cook chicken with red wine, or beef with white, and if you like to drink white wine with your beef, go right ahead. You have a perfect right to please your own palate, and you have lots of company.

to store: keep wines in a moderately cool place, the bottles lying on their sides so that the corks are kept wet and therefore expanded on the inside, not allowing air to penetrate.

TIP

- to store an opened bottle of wine, for use in cooking, pour the wine into a jar or bottle with a tight cover, since a cork which has been removed with a corkscrew may allow the wine to seep out, but certainly admits oxygen. Wine placed in a jar will keep well for cooking if it is used within about 3 weeks after opening. Don't refrigerate, for this may ruin the bouquet.

to chill: cool a wine (such as a dry white or a rosé) for a short time before serving. You may refrigerate it for an hour or two. Don't place it in the refrigerator in the morning for drinking at dinner; the flavor will be impaired. Red wines are generally served at room temperature except in hot weather, when you may chill them slightly.

to handle: be gentle with wine bottles prior to opening, having a care especially not to stir up any dregs.

in cooking: don't use any wine in cooking which you would not also enjoy drinking. A poor wine will bestow its poor flavor on the food.

TIPS

- any dish or sauce containing wine should be simmered uncovered until the alcohol has boiled off. If you smell alcohol, cook (slowly) some more.
- meats which are to be cooked with wine are generally better if they are browned first; searing keeps them from becoming wine-soaked. Wine-soaked meat does not usually taste good.
- a small amount of sherry is always excellent when cooked with shellfish, in creamed dishes, or added to consommé.
- dry vermouth, which is full-flavored, is excellent for chicken, but very little other seasoning is needed: vermouths contain many roots and herbs and are more full-bodied than other dry white wines. You also need less than if using other types of wine.
- if a wine sauce or gravy is too tart, add a few slices of carrot to the cooking pot. These may be removed before serving.

if wine begins to sour: don't try to use it in cooking. Let it go all the way, and become wine vinegar for use in salad dressings, etc. Wine which begins to sour is no longer wine.

Y

YAMS (see SWEET POTATOES)

YEAST: one envelope of active dry yeast (sold dated) can be used interchangeably with one cake of compressed yeast, but should be set to soften according to directions on the package. Compressed yeast (not too often found these days) has a shorter shelf life and is active for about a month after purchase. Both should be kept under refrigeration.

- brewer's yeast has no leavening power and cannot be used in baking.

in cooking: remove yeast from the refrigerator a couple of hours before using. It is less active when cold.

YEAST DOUGH (see BREAD)

PART TWO

•

Definitions of Cooking and Menu Terms

INCLUDING MANY ITEMS FROM THE INTERNATIONAL REPERTORY OF CUISINE

DEFINITIONS OF COOKING AND MENU TERMS

A

Agnello (It.): lamb

Aïoli (It.): containing garlic mayonnaise

Albert (Fr.): a hot horseradish sauce

Algérienne (Fr.): a garnish of small tomatoes and sweet potato croquettes

Allemande (Fr.): a rich cream sauce with egg yolks

Amandine (Fr.): containing almonds

Américaine (Fr.): a sauce or garnish containing lobster meat

Anglaise (Fr.): simple English-style cooking, such as boiling or steaming

Antipasto (It.): appetizer, hors d'oeuvres

Apfel (Ger.): apple

Arlésienne (Fr.): rings or slices of vegetables cooked in oil

Arm steak: a steak cut from the chuck (which see) requiring rather long slow cooking

Arroz (Sp.): rice

Aspic: a dish served in jellied form, or with a jellied garnish

Aurore (Fr.): a pink cream sauce, colored with paprika or tomato

B

Baba (Fr. & It.): a sweet yeast cake, soaked with rum or kirschwasser

Bagel: a hard, glazed, doughnut-shaped roll

Bain Marie (Fr.): a hot water bath used to keep foods warm

Bake: to cook by dry heat in the oven

Baron (of beef or lamb) (Fr.): the two legs and saddle cooked as a unit

Baste: to moisten occasionally with liquid while cooking or marinating

Bâtarde (Fr.): a butter sauce made with egg yolks

Bavarian: a rich cream pudding made with eggs, heavy cream and flavorings

Béarnaise (Fr.): a sauce for grilled meats made with wine, egg yolks, butter and herbs

Beat: to mix thoroughly with a rapid over-and-over motion

Béchamel (Fr.): a thick white sauce made with butter, flour and milk

Bercy (Fr.): a sauce with white wine and shallots as a base

Beurre manié (Fr.): a piece of

butter with flour thoroughly pounded into it, used as a thickener for a sauce

Beurre noir (Fr.): a tart sauce made with browned butter mixed with vinegar

Bigarade (Fr.): a sauce, usually served with duck, which includes orange juice and orange rind

Binding: a method of making particles of food adhere to one another, usually involving the use of eggs or flour

Bisque (Fr.): a creamy soup made from shellfish; also, a frozen creamy dessert

Blade steak: the same as Arm steak (which see)

Blanch: to pour boiling water over food, followed by rinsing in cold water

Blanquette (Fr.): a stew served with a cream sauce

Blend: to mix two or more ingredients together until smooth

Blini (Russ.): small unsweetened pancakes, often made with yeast

Boil: to bring a liquid to 212° F., when it bubbles constantly

Bombay duck: a small dried fish served in curry sauce

Bombe (Fr.): a rich dessert containing cream or custard

Bonito (Sp.): a species of small tuna fish

Bonne femme (Fr.): cooked home-style; often with a creamy mushroom sauce

Bordelaise (Fr.): a dark wine sauce made with pork, vegetables and garlic

Borscht (Russ.): a name used for two kinds of red soups: one made with beets, the other with tomatoes, cabbage and meat

Bouillabaisse (Fr.): a fish soup or stew containing many kinds of fish and shellfish, flavored with saffron

Bouillon (Fr.): a clear stock or broth made of meat, vegetables and seasonings

Bouquet garni (Fr.): a combination of herbs tied together, used as a flavoring in cooking, then removed

Bourgogne, Bourguignonne (Fr.): a highly seasoned brown sauce made with red Burgundy

Braise: to sear in fat, then cook gently, covered, in a small amount of liquid, usually in the oven

Bretonne (Fr.): an Espagnole sauce (which see) with onions

Brioche (Fr.): a large light sweet yeast roll

Brisket: the chest portion of the beef, usually extending some distance back of the forelegs; flavorful but rather tough, thus used in pot roasts and for braising

Brochettes (Fr.): skewers

Brodo (It.): broth

C

Café (Fr.): coffee

Café au lait (Fr.): coffee with hot milk

Calamares (Sp.): squid

Canapés (Fr.): bits of toasted or untoasted bread, or crackers, covered with various spreads, usually served with drinks

Canard (Fr.): duck

Caneton (Fr.): duckling

Cannelloni (It.): large tubular-shaped noodles, usually served stuffed

Cannoli (It.): ricotta-filled pastry

Capers: green hyssop buds used for flavoring sauces; sold packed in vinegar or in salt

Capon: a castrated young rooster, specially fed to yield tender meat

Caramel: a syrup made of sugar heated until it is melted and browned slightly

Carbonade (Fr.): braised or grilled or (sometimes) stewed meat

Carne (It. & Sp.): meat

Casserole: a meat, fish and/or vegetable dish which is cooked and served in the same (usually earthenware) pot

Cassoulet (Fr.): a dish of white beans cooked with meat

Castor sugar: a very fine granulated sugar

Caviar: the eggs (or roe) of sturgeon; also used to designate the roe of other fish, such as whitefish or salmon

Celeriac: a European celery with a thick stem base, which can be prepared in the same way beets are

Chantilly (Fr.): a dish containing or served with whipped cream

Charcuterie (Fr.): prepared pork delicacies

Charlotte (Fr.): a molded gelatin and whipped cream dessert, often surrounded with cake

Chasseur (Fr.): a sauce made with white wine, mushrooms and shallots

Chateaubriand steak: a very thick fillet of beef, exceedingly tender and juicy, cut laterally from the tenderloin

Chaud-froid sauce (Fr.): a creamy white jellied sauce used for coating chicken or fish

Chicken steak: a small, very tender and flavorful steak cut from the shoulder blade

Chiffonade (Fr.): a dish served with shredded or finely minced herbs or vegetables

Chile (Sp.): a spicy dish containing chili peppers and beans

Choucroute (Fr.): sauerkraut

Chowder: a thick soup or a stew made of shellfish, fish or vegetables

Chuck: a cut of beef from the region of the shoulder, neck and upper back, slightly tough, thus used for braising and stewing, or for grinding into hamburger

Chutney: a mixture of cooked fruits, sugar, vinegar and spices, served as an accompaniment to meats

Clabber: milk which has soured to the point where it is thick and curdy, but not separated

Clarified butter: the upper portion, clear, liquefied and oil-like, of butter when it has been allowed to melt slowly and stand without heat until the solids have precipitated

Clarify: to strain out any solids; to make clear, as in soup stock

Club steak: a rib steak from the top portion of the short loin. The higher the rib, the larger the steak. Size depends on thickness of cut also, and may serve one or two; very tender and juicy

Cocotte (Fr.): a small straight-sided baking dish with a cover, used for cooking eggs (in a pan of hot water) in the oven

Coddled eggs: eggs which have been placed in rapidly boiling water and at once allowed to stand undisturbed for 10 to 15 minutes, in the cooling water; this results in the whites and yolks having the same degree of jellied firmness

Collop: a piece of meat tenderized by beating or slicing thinly

Compote (Fr.): a combination of sweetened stewed fruits

Condiments: pickled or spicy food flavorings

Consommé (Fr.): a very rich meat or chicken stock (bouillon) which has been clarified, usually with egg white; also, a clear bouillon which will jell when cold

Coquilles St. Jacques (Fr.): scallops

Corned: meat which has been cured with salt or brine

Côte (Fr.): chop or rib

Coupe (Fr.): a dish of ice cream

Court bouillon (Fr.): a seasoned liquid in which fish or shellfish is cooked

Cracklings: the crisp residue, usually of pork, left after the fat has been rendered; or the rind left when most of the fat of a roast has been melted off

Crawfish: the spiny lobster

Crayfish: small fresh-water lobsters

Cream: to beat with a spoon or mixer until softened, as butter

Créole: designating a type of New Orleans cookery; dishes à la Créole are often cooked with tomatoes and okra

Crêpes (Fr.): thin pancakes

Crevettes (Fr.): shrimps

Croissants (Fr.): crescent-shaped flaky rolls whose dough includes some puff paste

Croque-Monsieur (Fr.): French version of a grilled ham-and-cheese sandwich

Croquettes: a mixture of ground or chopped foods, shaped, then dipped in crumbs or flour, and fried

Croustade (Fr.): a light pastry shell

Croûtons (Fr.): diced bread, often lightly sautéed in oil, served with soup or as a garnish

Crown roast: a ring of rib chops, usually lamb or pork, which is roasted in one piece, the center filled with a mixture of chopped meat and vegetables

Crullers: pastry strips or twists, fried in deep fat

Crumpets (Eng.): disk-shaped yeast muffins, usually served toasted

Cube steak: a beef cut, usually top round or top sirloin, which is tenderized by a "cubing" process involving pounding with a special mallet or being run through a "cubing" machine

Cuisse (Fr.): the thigh or leg

Curry powder: a ground mixture of caraway, cardamom, cloves, coriander, ginger, pepper, turmeric, among others

Cut in: to use knives or a pastry blender to mix shortening into flour until the pieces of fat are of uniform size and distributed evenly

Cutlet: either a small rib chop or a small cut of meat of about the same size; also used for minced meats shaped like chops

D

Dampfbraten (Ger.): beef stew

Daube (Fr.): a cube of meat

Delmonico steak: sometimes called a shell steak; a tender cut from the short loin

Dente, al (It.): not too soft; offering a slight resistance to the teeth

Demi-glace (Fr.): a partially clear, heavy brown sauce

Demitasse (Fr.): a small cup of black coffee

Deviled: highly seasoned, often containing mustard; frequently topped with bread crumbs and grilled

Diable (Fr.): a brown sauce with shallots, white wine, vinegar and herbs

Diane (Fr.): a peppery sauce flavored with game essence, with added butter and cream

Ditalini (It.): diagonally cut thick tubular noodles, 2 to 4 inches long

Dredge: to coat a food, as with flour or sugar

Drippings: fats and juices left when meats are cooked

Dulces (Sp.): desserts, sweet dishes

Dust: to sprinkle lightly, as with sugar, crumbs, flour

Dutch oven: a heavy cooking pot, usually of cast iron or enamel-on-iron, with a heavy cover

Duxelles (Fr.): a mixture of shallots, parsley, onions and mushrooms chopped, then stewed down to dryness, stored and used as a flavoring in sauces

E

Eclair (Fr.): a small finger-shaped bun made of puff paste with a glacé icing, filled with custard or whipped cream

Ecrivisses (Fr.): crayfish

Enchiladas (Sp.): tortillas stuffed with meat

Endive: a choice tender salad green related to chicory

English chop: a double-rib lamb chop

Ensalada (Sp.): salad

Entrecôte (Fr.): the same as Delmonico steak; a rib chop

Entrée (Fr.): originally, a meat or fish dish served before the main course; also used to designate the main dish of a meal

Epinards (Fr.): spinach

Escabeche (Sp.): pickled

Escallop: a thin slice of meat, poultry or fish; food baked in layers, covered with sauce and crumbs

Escargots (Fr.): snails

Espagnole (Fr.): a basic brown sauce made from veal and ham, from which many other meat sauces are made

Espresso (It.): strong black coffee made from specially roasted beans in a special kind of coffee maker

Estofado (Sp.): stew

Estouffade (Fr.): beef stew made with red wine

F

Faggot: a stalk of celery tied with parsley, bay leaf and thyme. Used in cooking soups, then discarded

Farce (Fr.): forcemeat

Farci (Fr.): stuffed

Farina (It.): a fine meal or flour

Fegato (It.): liver

Fettucine (It.): egg noodles

Filé powder: a powder made of dried sassafras leaves which has a glutinous quality and gives to certain dishes (as gumbos) a delicate flavor and thickening

Filet mignon (Fr.): a thick, boneless and extremely tender cut of beef from the tail side of the tenderloin. (Not, however, the most flavorful of steaks.)

Fillet: a slice; also, any steak served without the bone

Fines herbes (Fr.): a combination of very finely chopped herbs, usually parsley, tarragon, chives and chervil

Flambé (Fr.): served flaming, accomplished by pouring spirits over food and igniting them

Flan (Fr.): a tart, usually with a custard-type filling

Flank steak: the triangular-shaped muscle from the underside of a flank of beef; when broiled, served rare and sliced thin, as horizontally as possible, this is tender and juicy, and is called London broil. Flank steak is also served with a stuffing, rolled and baked

Flan ring: a metal pan for baking tarts, with low sides and a detachable side ring

Fleisch (Ger.): meat

Florentine (Fr.): a garnish, sauce, etc., which includes spinach

Foie (Fr.): liver

Fold in: to combine one ingredient with others in a gentle rolling motion

Fondue (Fr.): a well-beaten, then baked dish, usually including bread or cracker crumbs

Forcemeat: a rich, highly seasoned paste containing meat or fish, herbs and vegetables finely minced and pounded, used as a stuffing or garnish

Formaggio (It.): cheese

Fraises (Fr.): strawberries

Frappé (Fr.): sweetened fruit juices frozen until semi-hard, then chilled

French chop: a rib lamb chop

French fry: to cook in hot fat which entirely covers the food, usually in a special wire basket

Fricassée (Fr.): meat cut into small pieces and stewed, served with thickened gravy

Fritter: a small amount of batter which is fried in deep fat or sautéed, usually containing other ingredients which give their name to the fritter: as kernels of corn, any kind of berry, fruit, etc.

Fritto (It.): fried

Fromage (Fr.): cheese

Fry: to cook in hot fat which is fairly deep

Fumet (Fr.): a concentrated fish stock

Fumet, au (Fr.): consommé flavored by additional cooking with a vegetable or herb, often celery

Funghi (It.): mushrooms

G

Galantine (Fr.): cold, boned chicken or meat, shaped and chilled and served with a covering of aspic

Galette (Fr.): a crisp roll; a thin round unsweetened cake

Gallina (It. & Sp.): chicken

Gans (Ger.): goose

Garni (Fr.): garnished

Garnitures (Fr.): garnishes

Gâteau (Fr.): cake

Gazpacho (Sp.): a cold vegetable soup

Geflügel (Ger.): poultry
Gefüllte (Ger.): stuffed
Gehackte (Ger.): chopped
Gelati (It.): ice cream
Gelé (Fr.): jellied; iced
Gem: a muffin; hence, Gem pan: a muffin pan
Gemüse (Ger.): vegetables
Génevoise (Fr.): a sauce for fish made from a special white roux
Génoise (Fr.): a cold mayonnaise sauce made with nuts and cream
Giblets: the neck, heart, liver and gizzard of a bird
Glace (Fr.): ice or ice cream; also a concentrated meat stock
Glacé (Fr.): iced
Glaze: to cover with aspic or any shining covering, as jelly; also a concentrated meat stock
Gnocchi (It.): dumplings
Goulash: a Hungarian stew, usually quite thick
Gras (Fr.): fat
Gratin, au (Fr.): a dish covered with bread crumbs and butter or cheese, baked or placed under the broiler
Gratinée (Fr.): served with a bread crumb or cheese topping
Grenouilles (Fr.): frogs, frogs' legs
Griddle: a flat metal surface with a handle, for making pancakes, etc.
Grill: to broil
Grillade (Fr.): an individual serving of round steak, usually top round, and usually broiled
Grits: the dried kernels of hominy (made from corn)
Groats: the dried kernels of wheat or oats
Guacamole (Sp.): a paste of avocado, onion and spices
Gugelhopf (Ger.): a yeast coffee cake
Gumbo: a thick New Orleans Creole soup or stew containing either okra or filé powder as the thickening agent

H

Haggis (Scot.): a steam pudding made of finely minced sheep heart, lungs and liver
Hamburger: ground meat, usually beef, shaped into large patties and either sautéed or broiled
Hard sauce: a sweet white sauce made with butter, sugar and lemon juice, chilled until thick, served as a dessert topping
Haricots (Fr.): butter beans; navy beans
Hasenpfeffer (Ger.): rabbit stew
Hazelnuts: commercially, filberts
Hoe cakes, also known as johnny cakes: pancakes made with cornmeal
Hollandaise (Fr.): a thick yellow sauce made with egg yolks, butter and cream
Homard (Fr.): lobster

Hominy: hulled, split, coarsely ground corn

Hors d'oeuvres (Fr.): foods served before or as an introduction to the main meal; appetizers

Hot cross buns: sweet yeast buns with currants, slashed crosswise before baking, then glazed as they come from the oven

Hot-pot: mutton and vegetable stew

Huevos (Sp.): eggs

Huîtres (Fr.): oysters

I

Imbottito (It.): stuffed

Indian cress: nasturtium leaves and flowers, used in salad

Insalata (It.): salad

Irish stew: a stew including mutton and vegetables

J

Jambalaya: a combination of rice with meat or fish and/or vegetables

Jambon (Fr.): ham

Jardinière (Fr.): served with diced vegetables

Jerusalem artichoke: no relation to the true (globe) artichoke, but a pleasant-tasting tuber, slightly sweet

Johnny cakes: see Hoe cakes

Julienne (Fr.): food cut into matchlike strips

Jus (Fr.): strong meat stock or gravy

Jus, au (Fr.): meat served with its natural juice

K

Kaffee (Ger.): coffee

Kaffeekuchen (Ger.): coffee cake

Kale: a variety of cabbage with coarse curled leaves which can be cooked like spinach or used in salads

Kartoffeln (Ger.): potatoes

Käse (Ger.): cheese

Kebobs (Turk.): meats and vegetables arranged and broiled on skewers

Kedgeree (Anglo-Ind.): a rice and fish dish

King, à la (Fr.): food served in a cream sauce, often on toast

Kipper: salted, smoked herring

Kirsch (Ger.): cherry liqueur, often used in fruit sauces

Knead: to work dough with the hands, folding over, pressing down and turning repeatedly

Knödel (Ger.): dumpling

Kohlrabi: a member of the cabbage family, mostly grown for its base stem which is cooked much like turnip

Krusten (Ger.): pastries

Kuchen (Ger.): cake, usually yeast cake

L

Lachs (Ger.): salmon

Lait, au (Fr.): food prepared with milk

Langouste (Fr.): crawfish

Langoustines (Fr.): prawns, similar to shrimp

Langue (Fr.): tongue

Lapin (Fr.): rabbit

Lard: to cover with strips of fat, or to insert fat strips into meat with a larding needle

Lasagne (It.): very wide noodles

Leavening: yeast, baking powder, baking soda, or any substance which acts to make dough light

Leber (Ger.): liver

Leche (Sp.): milk

Leek: a pleasant-flavored green onion with very wide leaves, used in soups and stews or as a vegetable

Légumes (Fr.): vegetables

Lemon sole: a small flat fish resembling sole or flounder

Linguini (It.): narrow noodles

Livornaise (Fr.): a sauce made with olive oil, egg yolks and anchovy paste

London broil: see Flank steak

Lox: smoked, oiled salmon

Lyonnaise (Fr.): served or cooked with onions, or with an onion sauce

M

Macaroni (It.): a general name for the pastes which are made into various shapes and sizes, as spaghetti, linguini, vermicelli, etc.

Macaroons: cookies made of almond paste

Macédoine (Fr.): a mixture of cut-up vegetables or fruits

Madeleines (Fr.): small scallop-shaped cookies

Madère, au (Fr.): made with Madeira wine

Madrilène (Fr.): a clear chicken consommé flavored with tomato juice

Maïs (Fr.): corn

Maître d'hôtel (Fr.): a dish flavored with a butter sauce containing parsley and lemon juice

Mandel (Ger.): almond

Manicotti (It.): rolled pancakes stuffed with cheese

Maquereau (Fr.): mackerel

Marchand de vin (Fr.): a dark brown sauce made with meat and wine

Marguery (Fr.): a Hollandaise sauce made with shellfish essence and wine

Marinade: a mixture of oil, lemon juice or vinegar or wine and spices used to tenderize or flavor foods by soaking

Marinara (It.): a spicy tomato and garlic sauce

Mariné (Fr.): pickled, marinated

Marmalade: a preserve of oranges and sugar

Marmite (Fr.): a rich meat soup or stock

Marrons (Fr.): chestnuts

Marzipan: almond paste

Mask: to cover completely, as

with mayonnaise, jelly, aspic, etc.

Matelote (Fr.): fish stew; a sauce made with court bouillon and red wine

Mayonnaise: a sauce made with olive oil, egg yolks and vinegar or lemon juice

Médaillon (Fr.): the "eye" of a rib lamb chop

Meringues: egg whites and sugar beaten until stiff, then baked

Meunière à la (Fr.): fish or seafood sautéed and served in brown butter

Miel (Fr. & It.): honey

Mignon (Fr.): very small pieces, usually of meat

Milch (Ger.): milk

Mille feuilles (Fr.): a puff-paste pastry of many flaky layers

Mince: to cut up into very fine pieces

Mincemeat: a finely chopped mixture of apples, raisins, spices and suet, with or without a small quantity of meat

Minestrone (It.): vegetable soup, including some form of pasta (macaroni) instead of potatoes

Minute steak: a tender and juicy very thin steak cut from the top round, which can be quickly sautéed, broiled or pan-broiled

Mirepoix (Fr.): mixed vegetables diced very small and cooked with diced ham, used as a garnish

Mocha: the flavor resulting from the mixture of chocolate and coffee

Mode, à la (Fr.): food which is braised; also, pies and cakes served with a garnish of ice cream

Monaco, à la (Fr.): served with a green pea and caper sauce

Monosodium glutamate: known also as "Accent," a powder which "sharpens" the taste buds of the tongue, making it temporarily more sensitive to flavors

Mont blanc (Fr.): a rich dessert of chestnut purée and whipped cream

Montmorency (Fr.): a sauce made with cherries; also, a garnish made with artichoke hearts

Mornay (Fr.): a sauce similar to Béchamel, but with cheese

Moules (Fr.): mussels

Moussaka (Turk.): a baked lamb and eggplant dish

Mousse (Fr.): a dish made with whipped egg whites or whipped cream, often frozen; also, a molded finely ground meat, fish or vegetable dish

Mousseline (Fr.): a Hollandaise sauce to which whipped cream is added; also, a bubbly, light dish of finely ground meat or fish, often made with eggs

Moutarde (Fr.): mustard

Mouton (Fr.): mutton

Mozzarella (It.): a mild yellow cheese which melts easily

Mulligatawny: an East Indian curry soup, made of chicken or meat

Muscoli (It.): mussels

Mutton: the flesh of sheep over one year old

N

Nasturtium: see Indian cress

Navarin (Fr.): a stew of browned lamb

Nectarine: a smooth-skinned variety of peach

Nesselrode: a dessert or sauce with rum and fruit flavor, often with chestnuts

Newburg: served with a hot cream sauce containing sherry and pieces of lobster

Niçoise (Fr.): a garnish of garlic, tomatoes, capers and lemon

Noci (It.): nuts

Noisette (Fr.): a boneless chop, usually lamb

Noix (Fr.): nut

Normande (Fr.): a cream sauce containing fish essence, mushrooms and egg yolks

Nouilles (Fr.): noodles

Nudeln (Ger.): noodles

Nusskuchen (Ger.): nutcake

O

Oatcake: a flaky, flat Scots biscuit made with oatmeal

Oeufs (Fr.): eggs

Oie (Fr.): goose

Oignon (Fr.): onion

Okra: a kind of bean whose pod contains a gelatinous substance, used as a vegetable or for thickener in stews and soups (see Gumbo)

Olio (It.): oil

Orientale (Fr.): an Américaine sauce with added cream and curry powder

Ortolans (Fr.): tiny game birds (buntings)

Osso buco (It.): braised veal shin

Oyster plant: an edible root, known also as vegetable oyster, or salsify. It is prepared like parsnip.

P

Paella (Sp.): a dish of rice, chicken, seafood and vegetables

Pain (Fr.): bread

Panaché (Fr.): mixed

Panada (It.): a floury or soaked-bread paste, used in soups for thickening

Pan-broil: to cook quickly in a hot skillet with very little fat or a sprinkling of salt

Pane (It.): bread

Panettone (It.): a fruit-filled yeast cake

Panna (It.): cream

Papillote, en (Fr.): baked in an oiled paper bag

Parboil: to cook partially in boiling water

Pare: to remove the outer skin

or peel from fruits or vegetables

Parfait (Fr.): a dessert containing ice cream and whipped cream and hot or cold syrup, served in layers in tall glasses

Parfum (Fr.): flavor

Parisienne (Fr.): a white sauce with egg yolks

Parmentier (Fr.): any dish prepared with potatoes

Parmigiana (It.): prepared with Parmesan cheese

Pasta (It.): macaroni; any form of spaghetti or noodles

Pasticceria (It.): pastry

Pasticcio (It.): pie

Pastina (It.): tiny bits of noodles

Patatas (Sp.): potatoes

Patate (Sp.): sweet potato

Pâté (Fr.): a paste

Pâté de foie gras (Fr.): a paste made of finely ground goose livers

Pâtes (Fr.): pasta

Pâtisserie (Fr.): pastry

Paupiette (Fr.): thin-sliced chicken or meat, filled and rolled

Paysanne (Fr.): a dish prepared country-style; a vegetable garnish

Pêche (Fr.): peach

Pêche Melba (Fr.): peaches served with a raspberry sauce

Peperoni (It.): made with peppers

Perciatelli (It.): long macaroni

Périgeux (Fr.): a brown sauce made with Madeira wine and truffles

Périgourdine (Fr.): a Périgeux sauce with added goose liver

Persil (Fr.): parsley

Pesce (It.): fish

Petit pain (Fr.): a roll

Petits fours (Fr.): small iced cakes

Petite marmite (Fr.): a rich meat and vegetable soup

Pfeffer (Ger.): pepper

Pfeffernüsse (Ger.): peppernuts; small spicy cake balls, dusted with confectioners' sugar

Picadillo (Sp.): hash

Piccata (It.): chopped meat

Pignoli (It.): pine nuts

Pilaf, Pilau: an Armenian, Greek or southern Russian rice dish prepared with meat and vegetables

Pilze (Ger.): mushrooms

Pimento: sweet red pepper

Pin bone steak: a steak cut from the sirloin

Pintade (Fr.): guinea hen

Pipe: to push through a pastry tube to make a decorative line, as with mashed potatoes, cake icings, etc.

Piquante (Fr.): spicy, sharp

Pissaladière: a French version of Italian pizza

Pizza (It.): flat baked dough covered with various combinations of tomatoes, olive oil, anchovies, sausage, cheese, etc.

Plank: an oiled, grooved hardwood platter, usually oak, on which meat is served and carved

Poach: to cook in a hot liquid, just below the boiling point

Poire Hélène (Fr.): cooked pears with ice cream and chocolate sauce

Poisson (Fr.): fish

Poivrade (Fr.): made with pepper

Polenta (Sp.): a cornmeal dish

Pollo (Sp.): chicken

Pomidoro (It.): tomato

Pomme (Fr.): apple

Pomme de terre (Fr.): potato

Pone bread: corn bread

Porridge: hot oatmeal cereal

Porterhouse steak: a steak cut from the thick end of the tenderloin, or short loin, of beef

Potage (Fr.): soup

Pot-au-feu (Fr.): a combination of stock with meat, bones and vegetables, cooked together but often served as separate courses

Pot roast: beef cooked in a manner similar to braising, but on top of the stove

Pots de crème (Fr.): small custards, variously flavored

Poule (Fr.): chicken

Poulet (Fr.): young chicken

Praline (Fr.): burnt almond

Prawns (Eng.): for culinary purposes, the same as shrimp. In this country, large shrimp are sometimes called prawns. The true prawn is a small shellfish closely related to the shrimp, but it is European

Profiteroles (Fr.): small puff pastries filled with whipped cream or custard, covered with sauce

Prosciutto (It.): very thin slices of Italian smoked ham

Provençale (Fr.): served with a spicy garnish of tomatoes, mushrooms and garlic in oil

Puerco (Sp.): pork

Puff paste: a very rich dough containing a high percentage of fat, made light by entrapping air during mixing

Pumpernickel (Ger.): a coarse black bread made with rye flour

Purée (Fr.): food, usually cooked, forced through a sieve or ground in a blender. If a soup, a purée is thinned with stock or cream

Q

Quark (Ger.): cottage cheese

Quenelles (Fr.): forcemeat made into dumplings, then poached

Queso (Sp.): cheese

Quiche Lorraine (Fr.): a custard pie containing cheese and ham or bacon

Quohog, or **quahog:** the hard-shelled clam

R

Ragoût (Fr.): a rich stew

Ramekins: individual dishes in which food is browned and served

Ratatouille (Fr.): a tomato, eggplant and onion stew

Ravigote (Fr.): a velouté sauce with added onions, herbs, white stock and vinegar; served hot or cold

Ravioli (It.): stuffed and cooked "envelopes" made of noodle dough

Razor clam: a long, thin, razor-shaped clam, considered one of the most delicious of clams; eaten raw or cooked

Reduce: to boil down to make stronger and richer

Reis (Ger.): rice

Rémoulade (Fr.): a creamy salad dressing containing hard-boiled egg yolks

Render: to melt animal fat until the liquid portion can be removed

Rib steak: a steak cut from the rib portion, that part of the beef from which the standing rib roast or rolled rib roast is also taken; a club steak

Ricotta (It.): a sheep's milk cheese, similar to cottage cheese

Rigatoni (It.): ribbed macaroni

Rind, or rindfleisch (Ger.): beef

Ris (Fr.): sweetbreads

Roast: to cook uncovered in the oven

Robert (Fr.): a spicy brown sauce containing onions and vinegar, served with game and other meats

Roe: fish eggs

Roggenbrot (Ger.): rye bread

Rognoni (It.): kidneys

Rognons (Fr.): kidneys

Rosbif (Fr.): roast beef

Rôti (Fr.): roast

Round steak: meat from the thick central portion of the hind leg

Roux (Fr.): a thickener, made with fat and flour, for gravies

Russe, à la (Fr.): served with sour cream

Rutabaga: a yellow turnip-rooted cabbage; also known as Swedish turnip

S

Sabayon (Fr.): a dessert sauce made with egg yolks and Marsala wine

Sachertorte (Ger.): a rich chocolate cake

Saddle: the undivided loins of an animal, roasted as a unit

Saffron: the stigmas of the autumn crocus: a fine and delicate flavoring, used also to add yellow color to rice and other dishes

Salisbury steak: a restaurant term for quality hamburger, made of chopped sirloin

Salmagundi (Fr.): a mixture of many foods cut into pieces:

meat, chicken, seafood, cheese, vegetables, combined with or without a sauce, served cold

Salmis (Fr.): a fricassée or stew made from game birds

Salpiçon (Fr.): cooked food cut into tiny pieces, usually as a filling for pastry

Salsa (It.): sauce

Salsify: see oyster plant

Saltimbocca (It.): a veal and ham dish cooked in butter

Saucisse (Fr.): a very small sausage

Saucisson (Fr.): sausage

Sauerbraten (Ger.): sweet and sour beef in gravy

Saumon (Fr.): salmon

Sauté: to cook slowly or brown in a small amount of fat, shaking the pan from time to time

Scald: to put food in water which has not quite reached the boiling point; to immerse food in boiling water for a short time

Scallop: see Escallop

Scaloppine (It.): veal slices pounded very thin

Scampi (It.): shrimps

Schnecken (Ger.): round yeast coffee cakes

Schnitzel (Ger.): veal cutlets

Schwarzbrot (Ger.): dark whole-grained bread

Schwein (Ger.): pork

Scones (Scot.): tea cakes, shaped like a quarter of a circle

Score: to make lengthwise gashes on the surface of food

Scungilli (It.): conch (a shellfish)

Sear: to brown the surface of a food quickly, either under a broiler or in a pan

Selle (Fr.): saddle (of lamb, veal, etc.)

Semolina (It.): the fine wheat meal from which macaroni products are made

Shallots: a delicate-flavored small onion with a garlic-like bulb

Shashlik (Turk.): skewered broiled marinated lamb

Shell steak: the same as Delmonico

Sherbet: a frozen mixture containing fruit juices, water or milk, to which various thickeners are added before freezing, such as egg whites or gelatin

Shirred eggs: eggs broken into shallow ramekins containing cream or crumbs, then baked or broiled until set

Shortbread: a cake or biscuit whose dough has a high fat content

Short-broiling: the same as parboiling or poaching

Shortening: fats or oils

Short loin: the tenderloin

Shred: to cut into very narrow strips

Simmer: to keep a liquid at just below boiling point

Sirloin steak: a juicy, flavorful cut of beef from the portion of the animal between the rump and the tenderloin

Skewers: long thin metal pins on which food is impaled for broiling

Skillet: a frying pan

Skirt steak: the diaphragm muscle, a little-known but delicious cut of beef, very tender and juicy if broiled quickly and served rare

Smitane (Fr.): an onion sauce made with sour cream

Soda bread: Irish bread; a baking-powder bread, or one made with sour milk and baking soda

Sopa (Sp.): soup

Sorbet (Fr.): sherbet

Soubise (Fr.): with a flavoring of puréed onion

Soufflé (Fr.): a light, frothy baked dish containing well-beaten eggs

Soy: a thin pungent brown sauce made from soy beans and flavorings

Spätzle (Ger.): a dumpling

Spider: a frying pan

Spiedino (It.): fried cheese with anchovy sauce

Sponge: the portion of dough in bread-making containing all or part of the yeast, to which are added the remaining ingredients

Spoon bread: a kind of baked cornmeal pudding

Springerle (Ger.): anise-flavored cookies or pastries

Spumoni (It.): ice cream made with fruits and nuts

Squab: a 12- to 14-ounce pigeon

Steak Diane (Fr.): a very thin steak

Steak tartare (Fr.): very lean beef, minced and served raw

Steam: to cook, covered, directly above boiling water so that the steam permeates the food

Steam-roast: to cook, covered, in the oven, directly above boiling liquid; a cross between roasting and braising

Stew: to cook slowly in a covered pot in a small amount of liquid; a mixture of meat and vegetables cooked in this manner

Stock: the liquid from cooked meats, fish or vegetables

Strasbourgeoise (Fr.): served with goose liver and truffles

Strudel (Ger.): a thin, almost transparent sheet of dough covered with nuts, fruits, etc., rolled, and baked

Suchet (Fr.): with a flavoring of carrot

Sucre (Fr.): sugar

Suet: the hard fat found around the kidneys and loins of beef, mutton or pork

Sultanas: a type of large raisins, originally Turkish

Suppe (Ger.): soup

Suprême (Fr.): a rich heavy cream sauce

Suprême de volaille (Fr.): breast of chicken

Sweetbreads: the thymus gland, usually; sometimes also applied to the pancreas, of calves or lambs

Swiss steak: a steak (usually bottom round, sometimes lean chuck) into which seasoned flour has been pounded before cooking

T

Tagliarini (It.): long, thin noodle strips

Tagliatelle (It.): flat noodles, wider than tagliarini

Tallarines (Sp.): noodles

Tamale (Sp.): a cornmeal mixture with minced meat and red pepper

Tart: a one-crust pie, usually filled with fruit or berries

Tartare (Fr.): a mayonnaise sauce containing finely chopped pickles and mustard

Tartufi (It.): truffles

T-bone steak: a cut from the center section of the tenderloin, directly in front of the porterhouse steak

Teigemüsse (Ger.): macaroni dishes

Tenderloin: that portion of the beef between the sirloin and the ribs; also known as short loin. Steaks from the tenderloin include the porterhouse and T-bone

Terrine (Fr.): finely ground meats or fish, etc.

Timbale (Fr.): a molded dish; a high-sided pie crust filled with cooked meat, fish or fruit

Tipsy cake, tipsy pudding: sponge cake soaked with sherry and brandy, covered with custard and almonds

Tomalley: the liver of the lobster

Tonno (It.): tuna

Torrone (It.): nougat candy

Torta (It.): tart

Tortilla (Sp.): an omelet

Tournedos (Fr.): small fillets of beef, or thin strips of steak

Tripe: a part of the third stomach of the cow

Truffles: a fungus related to the sponge mushroom, maturing underground. They can be white, pink, brown or black.

Truite (Fr.): trout

Truss: to tie up, as a bird, so that all parts will remain in place while cooking

Try out: to heat fat slowly until it liquefies and can be drawn off

Tunken (Ger.): sauces

Turnover: a fruit-filled pastry circle which is doubled over to the shape of a semicircle and baked

U

Ugli: an irregular-shaped citrus fruit resembling an orange; also known as a tangelo

Umido (It.): a stew

Uova (It.): eggs

Upside down cake: a cake made by arranging fruit in the baking pan, over which the batter is poured. When cooled, it is inverted so that the fruit is on the top

V

Vaca (Sp.): beef

Vacherin (Fr.): a dessert of ice cream and raspberry sherbet; also a chestnut dessert; also a dessert built on rings of baked meringues

Valencienne (Fr.): a sauce for rice containing tomatoes, mushrooms, meat strips and grated cheese

Vaniglia (It.): vanilla

Veau (Fr.): veal

Vegetable marrow: a tender egg-shaped gourd, usually served stuffed

Velouté (Fr.): an extremely smooth creamy sauce made by adding butter and cream to a white sauce

Venison: the flesh of deer

Verdura (It.): vegetables

Vermicelli (It.): exceedingly thin spaghetti

Véronique (Fr.): containing or garnished with green grapes

Vichyssoise (Fr.): a thick cold smooth soup made with potatoes and leeks

Vinaigrette (Fr.): a dressing made with oil and vinegar

Vitello (It.): veal

Vitello tonnato (It.): veal with tuna sauce

Vol-au-vent (Fr.): a small puff paste shell with various fillings

Vorspeisen (Ger.): appetizers

W

Watercress: an aquatic green with a sharp agreeable taste, used in salads and as a garnish

Whip: to beat air into a liquid until it becomes thick and frothy

White sauce: a sauce whose base is butter, flour and a liquid such as stock, milk or water

Whitebait: the young of the herring, very tiny, usually sautéed

Wiener schnitzel (Ger.): breaded, fried veal cutlets

Wild rice: a North American grass, cooked like rice and often served with game

Worcestershire sauce: a dark thin sauce made with tamarinds, anchovies and garlic

Wurst (Ger.): sausage

Y

Yam: sweet potatoes; also a variety of sweet potato with a deep orange-colored flesh, tenderer and less stringy than the common yellow sweet potato

Yautia (Sp.): sweet potato

Yeast: a fungus used as leavening in bread and cake dough. It begins to grow at a temperature of 98.4, releasing gas in the presence of moisture

Yorkshire pudding: a baked batter of flour, milk and eggs, with the addition of meat juices

Z

Zabaglione (It.): a light dessert made with well-beaten eggs and wine

Zingara (Fr.): a sauce made with white wine, meat glaze, mushrooms, ham and tongue, finely chopped and peppered

Zita: (It.): wide tubular macaroni

Zucca (It.): squash

Zucchini (It.): green summer squash

Zunge (Ger.): tongue

Zuppa (It.): soup

Zuppa inglese (It.): sponge cake soaked in wine or brandy, with a custard sauce; similar to tipsy cake

Zwieback (Ger.): a sweet, dry toast; also known as rusks